MEMOIRS

OF THE

PRINCIPAL EVENTS

IN THE

Campaigns

OF

NORTH HOLLAND AND EGYPT;

TOGETHER WITH A

BRIEF DESCRIPTION

OF THE

ISLANDS OF CRETE, RHODES, SYRACUSE, MINORCA, AND
THE VOYAGE IN THE MEDITERRANEAN.

BY

MAJOR FRANCIS MAULE,

LATE OF THE 2D, OR QUEEN'S REGIMENT, AND ON THE
STAFF OF THE SEVERN DISTRICT.

1816.

The Naval & Military Press Ltd

Published jointly by

The Naval & Military Press Ltd

PREFACE.

The writer of the following pages having been requested by his friends to publish his Journal of the Campaigns in North Holland and Egypt, and the Voyage in the Mediterranean, he has attended to their request, as far as in his power, in a brief description of those Campaigns, during the whole of which he was present with the army.

There is already a very good account published of the same Campaign in Holland, but not by an officer serving in the field. Also, two accounts of the Campaign in Egypt: one by an officer, who, from being generally at head-quarters, possessed

great

great advantages to enable him to furnish minute details; the other by an officer on the staff, but who, during the Campaign in Egypt, was attached to the division of the army who were stationary in the lines of Alexandria.

The author of this brief work cannot boast to have possessed such advantages; but, having marched through Egypt with his regiment, he has been enabled to cite many instances of remarkable events, which could not otherwise be made known.

He does not profess to enter into minute details of military movements, as at so distant a period the marches and countermarches of regiments and brigades must be wholly unnecessary and uninteresting. On the contrary, he, with very few exceptions, studiously avoids all mention of names and indi-

individuals, trusting that by such observance he may avoid all obloquy and censure on so material a point.

The Campaign in Holland having been very short, the description of it here is also brief. The principal features of it have only been delineated; and the author states only such facts and circumstances, of which, in the usual routine of duty in the field, he was an eye witness.

It will be seen, that a combination of untoward and unforseen events rendered the success of that Campaign impossible, even to an army twice the number of that which actually landed in Holland.

A short description has also been given of the memorable voyage of the army destined for Egypt, and of several of the Islands, which they visited in their passage to, and their return from, that extraordinary country.

ERRATA.

Page 3, line 5, *for* incessantly *read* instantly
15,   9, *for* I was *read* We were
30,   16, *for* amounted *read* amounting
81,   3, *for* Vetten *read* Petten
36,   7, *after* following *dele* comma
—,   8, *for* enchanted *read* enchanting
42, 20, *for* Vetten *read* Petten
44,   4, *for* Marmorica *read* Marmorice
45, line at bottom, *after* Valetta place a full point
54, 16, *for* twelve *read* three
57, 16, *after* and *put* inhabited
74, line but one from bottom *for* and *read* or
78,   2, *after* had *put* probably
96,   4, *for* Ramun *read* Kamsin
123, 13, *for* midst *read* middle
125, 12, *for* this *read* home
136, 15, *dele* are
172,   1, *for* to us *read* known to us
177, 20, *for* le *read* ce
178,   2, *for* socle *read* siege
183,   2 *dele* pendant un mois, *and insert* et
189, 11, *for* believe *read* understood
200, 14, *for* linis *read* cinis
242, 13, *for* Gonderia *read* Gonderic
244, 20, *after* Spanish *insert* language
245,   1, *for* have *read* had
261, 13, *for* toros *read* tauros

CONTENTS.

CHAP. I.

ARRIVAL of the Expedition at the Helder
—Battle of the Helder—Landing of the
Russian Army 1

CHAP. II.

Battle of the 19th of September—Retreat of
the combined Armies—Battle of Alkmaer
—Capture of Alkmaer—Retreat of Marshal Brune—Retreat of the combined
Armies 18

CHAP. III.

Sailing of the Expedition to the Mediterra-
terranean—Malta—Island of Crete—Marmorica Bay—Island of Rhodes 44

CHAP. IV.

Debarkation of the Troops under Major General Sir John Moore — Battle of the
13th of March—Battle of Alexandria—
Death of Sir Ralph Abercrombie 71

CONTENTS.

CHAP. V.

March to Rosetta—Fort St. Julian—Rosetta
—March of the Army—Pyramids—Ramin or Desert Wind—Mamelouks—Ruins
of the City of Memphis 96

CHAP. VI.

Grand Cairo — Capitulation of General
Belliard—Account of the Funeral of General Kleber—Return of the Army to Rosetta 165

CHAP. VII.

Conduct of an Officer in the French Army—
Surrender of Alexandria—Pompey's Pillar
—Tower of Pharos—Ruins of Alexandria 189

CHAP. VIII.

Departure from Egypt—Syracuse—Monastery—Description of the Country 215

CHAP. IX.

Minorca — Mahon — Citadella — Arrival at
Gibraltar........................ 236

CHAP. X.

Journey to Ronda—Town of Ronda—Bull
Feasts—Amusements—Spanish Customs 257

CHAP. XI.

Return to Gibraltar — Description of the
pestilential Fever in that Garrison 283

BRIEF ACCOUNT, &c.

CHAP. I.

Arrival of the Expedition at the Helder—Battle of the Helder—Landing of the Russian Army.

THE armament destined for the attack upon North Holland, in the year 1799, sailed from the Downs, and the ports adjacent, in the month of August, under the order of Admiral Mitchell, and, after an unfavourable passage of a fortnight, reached the shore of the Helder.

B   The

The land forces upon this occasion were entrusted to Major-General Sir Ralph Abercrombie, an officer of distinguished service and merit.

On the 27th of August, at two in the morning, the preparatory signal was made for the troops to land.

The enemy, although not discernible, were known to be posted in rear of the long range of sand hills, which stretch themselves to a very considerable length along that part of Holland, and were here distant about one hundred yards from the immediate point of debarkation.

After the necessary time employed in placing the troops in the flat-bottomed and other boats appointed to convey them, a signal gun from the Admiral's ship announced the moment

moment for the line of boats to make for the shore. It was an anxious and momentous crisis. A cannonade, tremendous and well supported, incessantly commenced from all the line of battle ships, frigates, and gun boats, and bomb vessels. One hundred pieces of cannon without cessation opened over the line of boats, and hurled defiance upon the hostile shore. The resistance which would otherwise have been made by the enemy, was, in consequence, comparatively small, few casualties took place previous to the troops quitting their boats.

The brigade, to which I was attached, was one of the first landed. I do not recollect that any men were killed or wounded in the boats. On advancing however to reach

the

the sand hills, well-supported vol-
lies of musquetry, and a continued
fire of light artillery, saluted us on
all sides.

The brigade, notwithstanding,
after an obstinate and sanguinary
resistance, gained by slow degrees
the heights, still harassed by a numerous enemy. At the very foot of
the hills, I passed over the dead
body of a Colonel of Dutch artillery: His name was De Luk. He
was the only officer of rank who
fell that day. Some soldiers were
depriving him of his sword and
epaulettes, when, at the same instant, several of them were killed by
musquet balls.

Our loss at this period became
serious. The enemy shewed some
detachments of cavalry, but could
not act.

The

The light artillery and howitzers amply compensated them upon this point. A furious cannonade obliged the leading divisions of the English to pause. They were overwhelmed with a shower of grape-shot, as were also the troops which were advancing by the sea side. Many officers and soldiers here lost their lives. Amongst the number, one well known to me, of the 2d or Queen's Regiment; an officer of very promising, and of excellent character.

The situation of the sand hills presenting but a narrow field for action, prevented the English General from forming an extended line.

Had such been adopted, the left flank would have been exposed

and

and in the air ; in other words,
it would have been cut off, and
very soon, in all probability, turned
by the enemy's cavalry. The brigades were, in consequence, obliged
to observe contracted movements,
and to follow each other in close
succession. Manœuvres to any
great extent were impracticable.

Howitzers, the best artillery which
can be employed against an army
seated on hills, were adopted by the
enemy on this occasion. The large
masses of the advancing brigades
afforded an excellent mark, and by
the elevation of the enemy's guns,
much loss was unavoidably sustained.

Two hours from the commence-
ment of the engagement, I passed
by Major General Sir James Pulte-
ney, who was wounded. He was
sitting

sitting on a sand bank, and was attended by a surgeon binding his arm : immediately afterwards I heard of the death of the chief engineer, Lieut.-Col. Hay.

The enemy continued to fight bravely, and made several brilliant charges. In all of these, the steady valour of his antagonist prevailed, and towards noon he fell back about four miles, leaving Sir Ralph Abercrombie, in position, between him and the Helder Fort.

The loss of the enemy on this occasion amounted to about one thousand men.

The whole force of the Dutch troops, consisted of six thousand men of all arms, and were commanded by an officer of talent and experience, the General Daendaels.

The

The weather was rainy, cold, and tempestuous; sad presage of the autumnal season in the humid and trying atmosphere of North Holland. Its fatal effects would necessarily soon become visible in an army exposed, and without camp equipage of any sort; and since that period, I have again witnessed still more its baneful ravages in the well remembered climate of Walcheren. It is the parent of those unhappy fevers which undermine, unnerve, and wither all the faculties of the hardiest frames.

At six in the evening of the 27th of August, the brigade were ordered to bivouac on the Sand Hills.

The morning of this campaign thus dawned propitious. We shall see ere its sequel, how much we have

to

to reflect upon the uncertainty and vicissitudes of warfare; but that nevertheless its cares, its hardships, and its privations, are oftentimes productive both of instruction, and of advantage.

On the 29th of September, the enemy being aware of reinforcements received by the English, fell back still further about two leagues, the left of their army still resting upon the sea, and occupying some strong villages, upon their right.

The army of Sir R. Abercrombie in consequence advanced, and took up a position three leagues in advance from the Helder.

In the mean time, accounts reached the head quarters of the capitulation of the Helder Fort, and the line of batteries commanding the

harbour,

harbour, to Major General Moore's
division, together with the surrender
of the whole of the Dutch Fleet.
It had perhaps been fortunate for
the army in general, had the operations of the war here terminated,
and had they embarked instantly,
accompanied by their splendid ac-
quisition, the Dutch Fleet.

Events afterwards took place,
which no human wisdom could fore-
see.

The Hollanders, instead of aiding his Royal Highness the Duke of
York, who soon afterwards assumed
the command of the army, rather
joined the enemy, or remained totally inactive in their towns and
homes.

They seemed to be wholly regardless of any thing but the in-
undation

undation of their country, which they dreaded.

It was given out in England, that the Dutch only waited the arrival of the English, to declare against and drive out the French troops and authorities.

To ascertain *that* point on this side of the water was not very difficult. Matters assumed quickly a very different complexion, and we were soon convinced that the English and their Allies the Russians must depend upon their own exertions, and upon them only. Add to this, the English army were in a country which, from its flat and marshy situation, was very difficult of passage for troops and artillery.

By cutting a few of the numerous dykes and canals, which intersect

B 6   this

this country at the distance of almost every fifty yards, the passage
of troops becomes intercepted and
extremely difficult.

The enemy, in effect, on every
side formed redoubts on all the
roads, and threw up batteries in
rear of every dyke; from various
quarters also they received strong
reinforcements of troops of all
arms, particularly from the different
garrisons of Ostend, Dunkirk, An-
twerp, and Brussels. These reinforcements they were enabled to
send more readily in consequence
of the success of their arms at that
critical period in other quarters.

The retreat of the Marshal Su-
varoff and his Russians from Italy,
and the celebrated victory of the
Marshal Massena at Zurich, accelerated

celerated and accomplished these movements.

Marshal Brune soon afterwards assumed the chief command of the French army in Holland, accompanied by the General Vandamme, and other officers of high military character.

A strong division of troops from England arrived opportunely to reinforce the army, and were immediately disembarked.

On the following morning these troops, composed chiefly of regiments which had received volunteers from the militia, took their station in the line, and shortly afterwards, H. R. H. the Duke of York arrived, and took upon him the command of the army.

Sept. 10. The army made some
movements

movements and took up a new line, having its advanced posts upon Schagen Burgh, a considerable town, and surrounded at short distances by numerous farm houses. The brigade, to which my regiment was attached, occupied this town and the environs, which afforded excellent quarters, and abundance of all species of provisions.

The arrival and debarkation at this crisis of 10,000 Russian troops of all arms, under the orders of Major General D'Hermann and D'Essen, formed a principal feature of the campaign.

From this moment, every one looked forward for offensive operations. The rich and opulent cities of Holland already opened themselves to our view. I was fortunate

in

in being present when the Russian division arrived at the lines. The head of the column, composed chiefly of grenadiers, defiled past the Commander in Chief at midday; and were well appointed, and made a fine and imposing appearance.

I was delighted with their firm and noble gait, their healthy and bronzed countenance, and that general appearance of hardihood, the result of exercise and temperate habits, which fully denoted them fit for the field, and the privations incident to warfare.

The appearance of such an ally naturally gave rise to high expectations. The great character which the Russians have always maintained in war, which every year
manifests

manifests itself still more conspi-
cuously, and the known bravery of
their nation in general, filled every
one with confidence.

It must be observed, however,
that with all these advantages and
preparations on the part of the
English, calculated to afford san-
guine hopes to the government at
home, the enemy in the mean time
were no less active and alert in
assuming a strong attitude of defence.

Reinforcements had already reached them, and others were continually leaving the Netherlands for
the same purpose. A line of country, extending from Oud Caespel to
Bergen, commanded by the heights
on the sand hills, which were occupied by a numerous artillery, presented an imposing aspect.

The

The canals and roads at various points were defended by formidable batteries, and ditches were cut in almost every direction, leading to their line of intrenchments.

CHAP. II.

Battle of the 19th of September—Retreat of the combined Armies—Battle of Alkmaer—Capture of Alkmaer — Retreat of Marshal Brune—Retreat of the combined Armies.

ON the morning of the 19th of September, at two o'clock, the combined army were under arms, and marched immediately. I recal to mind the anxiety of *that* march. The remembrance of this extraordinary and novel scene has not been obliterated by time, or even by other

other scenes equally awful and impressive. The recollection of these events, by which the lives of so many thousands were affected, afford sometimes an interesting subject of retrospection.

Leaving the high road from Schagen, the brigade, forming almost the left of the combined Russian and English army, defiled along the banks of the great canal of Alkmaer, and immediately directing itself upon the enemy's position at Oude Carspel.

The march of the troops was silent and uninterrupted. Towards day-break, the first discharge of cannon took place from the French line.

Immediately followed a rapid fire of light troops and riflemen, which

which was soon succeeded by a continuation of musquetry along the whole of the right and centre of the combined army. The cannonade from the French batteries was tremendous. The Russians meanwhile attacked the left of the enemy's position. An unparalleled fire of musquetry, resembling the roll of drums, seemed to overwhelm their opponents, who were embattled in the several villages, and who defended them with an excessive obstinacy and perseverance.

Battalions and squadrons, both Russian and English, proceeded at the same time against the main army, which was posted in the rear of a considerable dyke, intersected at various points, and flanked by several heavy and formidable batteries.

The

The difficulty of forcing such a position must be obvious. The attack here commenced, and continued with unexampled fury. Reinforcements became necessary, and were sent in support of this arduous operation.

Meanwhile, the cavalry from the rear deployed, for the purpose of attacking the villages and the points least defended.

The enemy had forseen this movement, and had availed himself of circumstances; continual rains, and the overflowing of several canals, rendered the ground extremely wet and marshy. The advance of the dragoons was thus impeded; and, upon their arrival at the villages, they found them defended by the inhabitants.

The

The result of the manœuvres and attack by the Russians was expected with impatience, its success being considered certain : but this was retarded by the obstinate resistance which the corps of Vandamme made to hold the villages which covered the left wing of their army. This wing defended the town of Bergen and the villages contiguous. They incessantly sent battalions to this point, and frequently repulsed the charges of the Russians.

Meanwhile, the left wing of the army, composed entirely of English troops, advanced towards the fortified position of the enemy at Oud Caespel, forming their extreme right.

Here they had constructed a principal redoubt and tete-du-pont. It was

was impossible to enter Oud Caespel, but by the occupation of this
formidable barrier, or to approach
by the canal of Alkmaer, which
runs parallel with the town. A gun
from this point preceded a heavy
and dreadful fire upon the leading
brigade. This attack fell heavy
upon those brave troops, and a very
considerable number of men and
officers lost their lives.

It was now mid-day. The enemy,
with an obstinacy unequalled, maintained himself until five in the afternoon.

A movement of some battalions,
which had halted in a wood, about
an half league distant, to cross the
canal and attack his rear, at length
obliged him to relinquish his strong
position. He accordingly fell back,
leaving

leaving the whole of his guns and a considerable quantity of ammunition.

The village, which we entered, presented a sad spectacle of the horrors of war. Numbers were found in the houses, as well as in the streets, extended upon the ground pierced with balls and otherwise severely wounded. Artillery and ammunition-waggons, with their ill-fated horses dreadfully lacerated by cannon-shot, with their drivers laying dead beside them, filled the streets at various points.

The regiment, at eleven *p. m.* were *en bivouac* in advance, near a windmill. Already had fatigue and sleep oppressed those not on duty for the night. It was a repose of short duration. An order, brought by an Aid-

Aid-de-Camp, escorted by dragoons from head quarters, caused a change in our destination. We marched immediately, no one knew whither, the officer commanding excepted. We proceeded, however, with rapidity ; and, in the space of an hour, found (by the moans of the wounded which were distinctly heard) that we were then approaching the scene of the terrible redoubt.

These, in fact, were the unhappy men, wounded by the enemy's fire in the morning attack, and who had been left on the field. Such, however, was the necessity of the retreat that not a man could be brought away. Several surgeons were left to assist them.

Amidst the rain, which fell in torrents, and a tempestuous wind, the

lamen-

lamentation of these poor men at intervals struck the ear. The hollow gale wafted after us their melancholy but unavailing cries. Our situation from inability to aid them was truly distressing.

We distinctly heard the voices of many, and the confused murmurs of the dying, who in prayer and supplication, were terminating both their pains and their existence: in other places were discovered horses with their legs broken by shot, laying on the spot where they had at first been wounded.

The apparent resignation and still position of these animals, whom we knew to be under the dominion and influence of excruciating pain, added to the pity which we had for them, and the extreme regret we experienced

perienced for their miserable situation.

The march of the brigade, followed by the cavalry, continued
rapidly. During the greater part
of the night, a heavy firing was still
heard upon the right in the line of
Bergen. This was no other than
the retreat of the Russians, whose
route was marked by the flames of
villages, which were at that fatal
period totally consumed. The
French General, Vandamme, had
reoccupied Bergen, from which he
had been driven in the morning,
and was now, in turn, in pursuit of
his assailants.

The roar of artillery warned us of
the proximity of the two parties;
and continued explosions filled the
air with frightful noises. On a sub-

sequent

sequent occasion, I was enabled to witness the devastation and ruin occasioned to the unhappy Hollanders in these once beautiful villages.

The all-devouring element had, in a few hours, swept away the produce of their unceasing labour, and desolated the whole face of this abundant and productive country.

The Dutch village surpasses perhaps in its neatness, its order, and in its general appearance, the villages either of Europe or any other part of the world. Every little farm in North Holland is well stocked with cattle, which are carefully defended from the rigours of winter in regular and well built stables, the whole of which are kept as cleanly as the parlours of England.

I never

I never have observed among the Dutch the least tendency to disorderly conduct. A peaceable disposition is universal throughout this rich and fertile country.

The carrillons of Schagen were already announcing the hour of four, when my regiment re-entered that welcome quarter.

From this period until the beginning of October, no event of importance occurred after the retreat of the 19th of September, occasioned by circumstances of which I am not sufficiently acquainted to speak. The army continued in the same position, as occupied by them before that unfortunate day.

It was given out that another attack would shortly take place, and preparations were made to that effect.

c 3

It

It will be necessary here to essay
another description of a second most
sanguinary battle on the 2d of October.

I was informed that a division of
troops, composed chiefly of the old
regiments, under the command of
Major-General Sir R. Abercrombie,
which, on the 19th of September,
had occupied Hoorne, and who were
thereby prevented from co-operat-
ing in the engagement on *that* day,
were now recalled to the main army.

This division, certainly composed
of the best troops of the army,
amounted to nearly eight thousand
men, according to report, were on
this day commanded by Sir Ralph
Abercrombie on the extreme right
of the Sand Hills. The brigade to
which the regiment was attached,
was also employed in that quarter.

At

At the point of day, I remember marching close to the village of Vetten. His Royal Highness the Duke of York was standing, surrounded by his staff, on a rising ground near the village from whence he saw the several regiments pass him in succession.

The most severe part of this day's contest fell upon the division of the army already mentioned, appointed to act on the Sand Hills, whose movements were both unforeseen and multiplied.

The enemy throughout the day maintained their military character, and fought worthy of themselves. The opposition made by them was very great, and the combat through-out hardly contested.

The day at length terminated in
the

the complete success of the Duke; the enemy's columns were observed retreating by the high road of Alk- maer, whilst they still employed some battalions to dispute the hills, and thereby facilitate the retreat.

We passed the night on the Sand Hills, the brigade occupying them in line from the sea side. Before morning, we were joined by officers of various regiments, some of whom had lost their way, and some who had been slightly wounded. We had also been joined during the day by nearly two hundred stragglers from the battalions of grenadiers and light infantry. Many of these men had left the regiments of militia a few weeks before in England.

At midnight the Prince of Orange came up; and laid by the fire wrap- ped

ped in his cloak. The weather was extremely wet and cold.

Early on the following morning, we were enabled to form some judgment of the still powerful numbers of the enemy, and consequently that he had not quitted his positions, without sustaining very great losses. I forbear to mention their amount, because such calculations are usually uncertain, and hazardous.

Although the enemy had yielded the field of battle, the country beyond *that* field, with the exception of the town, was totally in his power. The same difficulties existed. The country, even to the walls of Amsterdam, presented the same obstacles, and without doubt it was very soon perceived, that without very considerable reinforcements,

c 5   amounting

amounting in numbers perhaps to the strength of the existing army, the conquest of North Holland would be impracticable, and the object of the expedition consequently fail.

October the 3rd, the French army continued to retrograde. His long protracted columns, accompanied by a numerous field artillery, were plainly discerned defiling for an extent of several miles, along the Chaussee leading to Alkmaer, and even beyond *that* town. Other divisions were seen in retreat on the line of the sea shore. The army of the Duke moved forward at daybreak. My regiment at mid-day were quartered in a large Chateau or palace, situated in a spacious wood not far distant from Alkmaer. These

These quarters were indeed admirable, and afforded a striking contrast to what we had previously occupied, and to those which we were shortly afterwards destined to accept.

Rooms sumptuously furnished, gardens abounding with every thing, and skirted by a noble and umbrageous avenue of lofty trees of various kinds. In a superb and spacious saloon, I took notice of nearly forty paintings of the most celebrated masters; amongst them were Teniers, Vandyke, Rembrandt, and Wooverman.

In the gardens were several large collections of various shrubs, and botanical plants. These were found at several points of the inner garden, and produced the most delightful odours.

c·6   Circum-

Circumstances, however, did not
long permit us to enjoy this com-
parative paradise. It was the April
sunshine, and a deceitful calm. A
fatal succession of events shortly
awaited us in our career.

The morning following, our arrival at this enchanted palace, (for
such it appeared to me, who for the
month past had been accustomed
to ships, sand hills, and miserable
marshes) I employed in riding
through the wood, which embosoms
this delightful abode. It is enno-
bled by several avenues of very lofty
trees, and on one side a lake runs
parallel from the entrance gate of
the wood close to the palace.

At nine in the morning of the
5th October, we entered Alkmaer.
As the advanced guard of the brigade passed through the gates, the
sounds

sounds of the carrillons, for which Holland is celebrated, were particularly pleasing.

On subsequent occasions in this country, I have frequently listened to them with much satisfaction.

We had but a transient view of this fine town, remarkable for its superior neatness, many good buildings, and the delightful and regular walks which are laid out and continued, completely around it.

This evening we again bivouaced two leagues in front of Alkmaer. On the 6th, the morning loured; it seemed to presage an ill-fated change. A deep mist prevented the view of either friend or enemy.

Ere long, however, the ears of all acquainted them with the near approach of enemies, and those of the most formidable description. A heavy

A heavy cannonade burst forth
upon our right. I here understood,
but do not presume to declare further, that a feint attack was only
intended in order to ascertain the
actual force of the enemy, but that
a more general engagement became
unavoidable, in consequence of unforseen circumstances. Whatever
may have been the cause, a sanguinary battle ensued.

My regiment lost some men. At
4 p. m. an order was received to
retrograde: the enemy pushed us
with their tirailleurs, and light artillery. These last, were hurried
through the mud and water, in
which we stood, with incredible alacrity.

The French gunners accustomed
a long time in Germany and Italy,
to

to pursue, plied us with rare assiduity.

I remember the report to have
reached us, that on the right we
had suffered considerable loss, and
that a whole battalion of one regiment, one of the strongest in the
army had been surrounded, and
made prisoners by the enemy's cavalry.

Marshal Brune had received
strong reinforcements. We passed
the night in the midst of continual
rain, accompanied by a tremendous
gale of wind in the neighbourhood
of the village of Egmont op Zee.
The noise occasioned by this tempest
was so great, that until our actual
arrival, we did not hear any of the
clamour and confusion which reigned in every part of this apparently
wretched place.

Russians

Russians of all arms with their artillery, caissons, and other carriages, conveying away their sick and wounded, were seen in all directions. Every street and road appeared full of them. Many of the waggons carrying the wounded were without covering, and the unfortunate sufferers were seen rolled up in blankets drenched with rain, and disfigured with the marks of their blood. Still these noble and hardy soldiers appeared unmindful of their lot, and bore not in their stern and manly countenance the marks either of grief or of dismay.

On the 7th of October, at the earliest dawn, the brigade were under arms, and marched immediately, taking the sea-shore. The movement was retrograde.

The security which this route afforded

forded, was evident; but we were
dreadfully harassed by the deep and
heavy sands. The baggage horses
were frequently seen rolling over
with their oppressive and heavy burthens, and no inconsiderable number
ber of them as well as men, fell into
the hands of the enemy's hussars,
who followed close upon us, and
seized upon every weary straggler.

The weather and elements seemed
to conspire against us, and continued hostile during the whole of the
retreat. A powerful corps of cavalry hung upon our rear. These very
troops had, a few hours before, covered the retreat of their own
columns. No sooner, however, did
they perceive the unexpected retrograde movement of the combined
army, than they instantly changed
their route.

It

It must be confessed, the French generals and soldiers conduct themselves upon such occasions with a vigor and alacrity unparalleled, without heeding fatigues, dangers, or privations; they take advantage and avail themselves with astonishing rapidity of the weakness, the errors, or the misfortunes of their opponents.

The retreat continued orderly notwithstanding the unbounded fatigue during the whole of *that* day. Night also overtook us, weary almost to death by these continued marches, want of food, and the very worst of weather.

As we left this inhospitable and dreary tract, and defiled by the village of Vetten, a small advanced guard, commanded by a serjeant, mistaking the appearance of the canal

canal for the beaten road, precipitated themselves into the water.

They were fortunately rescued, and a general officer and his staff, who were closely following the steps of the guard, were barely saved from sharing in their disagreeable dilemma.

At two in the morning, we again arrived at, and re-entered Schagen Burgh; and, after the convention which speedily followed, the Army re-embarked for England.

CHAP.

CHAPTER III.

Sailing of the Expedition to the Me-
diterranean — Malta — Island of
Crete—Marmorica Bay—Island of
Rhodes.

IN the year 1800, in the month of
June, an expedition of considerable
strength, and under convoy of a numerous fleet of men of war, sailed
from England. I believe that
scarcely an individual in the army
embarked could form the most remote idea of his destination. They
continued many months confined
in their vile and insupportable pri-
sons,

sons, the transports wandering over the Atlantic and Mediterranean Seas.

My good fortune caused me to embark in the December following. The voyage was rapid, and by no means disagreeable. I arrived, in a frigate, in nine days off Cape Trafalgar, and the same evening anchored in the bay of Gibraltar. Here I had an opportunity of landing for one day, the whole of which was employed in examination of that extraordinary place. In after days, I had, unluckily, much more time and opportunity to perform *that* service.

On the twenty-first day from quitting England, the frigate reached Malta, two leagues distant from the harbour of Valetta, the gale which

had

had so rapidly wafted us up the
Mediterranean, increased considerably, and terminated with an accident. A flash of lightning carried
away the mizen-top-mast ; and with
it, a poor black sailor, who, but a
few moments before, had taken *there*
his ill-fated station.

In entering this noble haven, between the forts St. Elmo and St. Angelo, a boat, with musicians, according to their usual custom, met us,
and preceded the vessel. The music was simple, but, like all compo-
sitions of that latitude, extremely
pleasing.

Malta, situated between Europe
and Africa, is a stupendous fortress,
and presents the most formidable
aspect, both from its singular situation, and the numerous bastions,
forts,

forts, and ramparts, by which it is
surrounded and defended. According-
ing to the mode which I was resolved to adopt, to visit and explore
every thing which came in my way
in these classic regions, I procured
a guide to explain to me the curiosities of the place.

The church of St. John is a noble
pile ; the roof of which is decorated
with paintings, in fresco of Cala-
breze. The guide informed me,
that in the sacristy was a magnificent painting, by Michael Angelo
di Caravagio, but from some cause
I did not see it.

The library possesses many relics
of antiquity, and some vases of
beautiful workmanship, found at
Gozzo. We also visited the church
of St. Paul at Civita Vecchia, which
is

is magnificently ornamented, and surpassing every thing of the kind which I have seen. A few leagues from Civita Vecchia, we paid a short visit to the cave of St. Paul.

The fortifications, the harbour, and buildings of Malta are of the first description.

I have never seen in the ports of France, Spain, or England, any thing which may be compared to these extraordinary efforts of human labour. Nature has also combined with art, and rendered the military strength of this important fortress truly noble and magnificent.

The island of Gozzo, called by the poets the island of Calypso, is distant about two leagues from Malta.

If in the days of Homer this island

island was so delightful, so abounding in woods, ruins, and beautiful scenery, and the abode of a goddess, it has now lost its enchantment; and resembling the beautiful Calypso, has like her, proved itself not to be immortal. The grotto of the goddess, the verdant banks eternally covered with flowers, the trees which for ever in blossoms, overshadowed the baths of her and of her nymphs, have now entirely vanished.

The fleet, in which were embarked fifteen thousand troops, together with a battering train, and every species of military stores and equipment, at length sailed from Malta; under a numerous convoy of men of war.

A prosperous gale, in mild and serene weather, wafted us, in the

D   space

space of a few days, near the island of Candia or Crete.

Passing near the spot of the celebrated battle of Lepanto, I recalled to mind that day of exultation for all the Christian powers.

Here the skill and bravery of Don John of Austria, animated his followers to destroy the Turkish forces, equally powerful in arms as implacable in revenge.

These very Mahometans were now in alliance with the English nation, in order to drive away and destroy Christians of almost similar persuasion in religion, arts, and customs.

Such are the intricate and tortuous windings of political transactions.

From the early morning, the frigate

gate seemed to approach rapidly an
island of considerable extent. We
perceived at an immense distance
Mount Ida, the birth place of Jupiter; and, as we advanced, the
country gently undulating with ac-
clivities, presented an unbounded
verdure, with which it is covered
from the tops of the rising hills to
the very brink of the shore.

The delightful prospect added
new eagerness to our wishes to land.
We were now in sight of the very
country of Minos and of Radaman-
thus.

Homer thus speaks of Crete.

" Crete is an extensive island, in
the midst of the stormy main. The
soil is rich and fertile. It contains
an immense number of inhabitants.

We

We find their Achæans, Cydonians,
Dorians, and godlike Pelasgians."

Here we call to recollection the
names of Pasiphae and of Theseus,
of Ariadne and the Minotaur. From
hence also Idomeneus conducted
the Cretans to the plains of Troy.

Many celebrated poets also owed
their birth to Crete. The ravages
of time have deprived us of all their
works: their names only have de-
scended to posterity.

The hundred cities of Crete are
now no more. Nations are effaced
from the earth, like the monuments
of their power; and, after the revo-
lution of several ages, we can scarce
trace in their posterity any remains
of their ancient character. Some
of them exist longer, others for a
shorter

shorter time ; but all are doomed
to bear at last the yoke of a stronger and more fortunate neighbour.
Crete for a long time, and even previous to the period of which we have
any correct account, flourished in
unequalled splendour. At length,
the time arrived when the warlike
and victorious Romans aspired to
the empire of the world, and would
suffer none but their subjects or
slaves to inhabit within the reach of
their arms.

I must not here omit to say a few
words respecting Mount Ida, which
displayed itself in full majesty, as
the vessel slowly proceeded on her
way. To the westward of Candia
is an extensive range of hills, leading to and forming a communication
with Mount Ida.

Athough the Turks, who destroy every thing, and devastate wherever they go, have very much disfigured this beautiful country; yet beyond the extent of these hills the fields of corn, and orchards of fig-trees and vines are abundant.

The hand of industry is everywhere visible. Adjoining Mount Ida are also many high mountains, which diversify and ennoble the scene.

A writer of some eminence gives the following description of Mount Ida.

"Being about twelve hundred fathoms below its highest elevation, we enjoyed an agreeable temperature of the air. The sky was unclouded and serene; and the sun held its course through the azure vault

vault in all its dazzling pride. The streams, flowing through the deep vallies to our left, were overhung with myrtles and laurel roses. The foot of the mountain was adorned with green trees; and, in the month of November, we found arbours, whose verdure was fresh as if it had been spring."

On the eastern side of Ida, the country changes and presents a different aspect. The various landscapes, which successively attracted our attention, proved tenfold more enchanting to men long confined within the narrow compass of a ship. For the space of several leagues, we observed a continued verdure nearly touching the sea.

Beyond these are discovered forests of various description of trees;

and

and; indeed, on every side, you are
struck with the variety of beautiful,
rich, and splendid prospects.

The account given us of the climate of Crete is truly enviable. The
weather is generally mild, although
strong gales of wind frequently arise
in that latitude.

The inhabitants of Crete never
experience any of those piercing
colds which are so frequently felt in
our own regions, and which succeeding suddenly after the cherishing
warmth of spring, destroy the flowers and fruits, and are fatal to deli-
cate constitutions. Ten months in
the year, according to those who
have resided there the sky is unclouded and serene. The winds
are mild and refreshing breezes.
The nights, in this part of the world,
are

are no less tranquil. Their coolness is delicious. The atmostphere, not being overloaded with vapours, renders it at all times favourable to the traveller to pursue his journey or even to sleep in the open air.

On the 16th of January, at day break, it was observed that the Admiral had altered his course, and was steering for the sea of Marmora.

In the evening, we approached the island of Rhodes, formerly the abode of valour, of merit, and of honour, but now the resort of ignorance and barbarity, and by beings altogether uncivilized.

The entrance into the Straights, which conducts to the spacious Bay of Marmorice, is marked by the appearance of several large mountains.

We

We arrive at a narrow pass: as we
wind along these delightful banks
formed by mountains, towards the
mouth of the Bay, we catch a
glimpse of several villages romanti-
cally situated. These mountains
majestically arising above each other
in the figure of pyramids, whose
summits are crowned with myrtle,
orange, and citron trees, present a
charming and interesting scene.

Habitations indeed enviable, if
occupied by people very different
from their present possessors.

The Bay of Marmorice, our destined anchorage for some weeks,
completes a circumference of three
leagues, and is encompassed by hills,
covered with lofty trees, beyond
which are extended on every side
considerable forests and woods.

Every

Every day which I could snatch
from my prison, the transport, was
employed in excursions into the
country, and in the forests in the
vicinity.

In all these expeditions, great cir-
cumspection became necessary, to
guard against the beasts of prey,
wolves and leopards, which nume-
rously occupied the recesses of the
forests. At night we usually heard
the howlings of these animals, as we
lay on board the vessels. About the
distance of a mile from one of the
landing places, is situated a Turkish
village. Around it is a charming
country, refreshed and fertilized by
brooks and rivulets. The environs
are planted with lofty trees, and
embellished with luxuriant orchards
of fig trees, being enlivened also by

many

many neat houses, whose inhabitants seem occupied in the business
of prosperous cultivation.

As you cross the forest, the eye
discovers a small town, partly sur-
ounded by ruins, embosomed by
mountains of immense height. On
a rising ground immediately above
the town stands a mosque, the approach to which is directed by avenues of trees of the most luxuriant
foliage.

These avenues, four in number, are
of great length, through which the
votaries of Allah pass and repass in
constant succession. We purchased
here some honey of exquisite fla-
vour, resembling that of Minorca,
the bees feeding on the flower of
myrtle and orange trees. After the
first of these excursions, I had nearly

ly met with a serious accident in the Bay of Marmorice. The gales of wind here are sometimes very severe. Although the day had been unusually serene and tranquil, the evening sky presented a heavy and almost terrific aspect. We had in fact been overtaken mid-way between the shore and the ship, by a species of tornado or whirlwind, not unfrequent in those countries, which almost instantaneously drove back the boat towards the shore in spite of every effort. The violence of the wind soon occasioned a prodigious surf, and rendered its approach almost certain ruin: providentially, one vessel, a man of war, was at anchor not far distant, and became our aid and refuge in the moment of extreme danger.

On

On another occasion a small party
landed with me at day-break, and
proceeded with an intention of taking some sketches of the old ruins,
which are situated about three
leagues in a north westerly direction. We were provided with mules,
and two guides, and were all of us
well armed. After traversing a thick
forest of pines, olive, and other trees,
we arrived at a delightfully open
country, well cultivated, and occasionally interspersed with cottages,
and other buildings. The ruins of
a considerable palace or castle, gradually appeared as we advanced, and
large masses of decayed stone work.
At intervals pillars are seen of a
considerable distance: they plainly
attest the noble structure which
once graced this delightful spot, in
times

times perhaps when the followers of
Mahomet were held in more consideration than in the present æra.
The founder, like that of the more
celebrated pyramids, intended to
have made known to distant posterity, the splendour of his imagination, and the greatness of his
wealth and power

The environs are at certain distances ornamented with avenues of
trees, near which are also the relics
of other buildings. We perceive on
the other side the mountains of Asia,
which unfold themselves as we advance, and which form altogether
one of the finest prospects perhaps
in the world.

On our return to the bay in the
evening, in passing through the
thickest part of the wood, one of the
party

party shot at a leopard. The animal made a noise, and instantly made off, by which I conclude he may have received a wound. These animals continually lay in ambush, and dart upon the unwary traveller. Our retreat became in consequence a little more circumspect and even rapid, our guide having hinted to us the partiality of those gentry to reconnoitre at the approach of night.

On the day following, a boat calculated for the purpose, having been obtained, we by dint of labour and aided by a guide, reached the neighbourhood of Rhodes. The ruins of this once celebrated country, are still interesting to the attentive traveller, and afford objects worthy of inspection.

It is now no longer a place of any note ;

note ; although from its situation,
and being in the country where
wood is abundant for the construction of ships, it is well calculated for
the purposes of commerce. The
town is situated in the extremity of
a promontory, extending to the eastward, precisely in the same spot occupied by the great city. An ancient writer of great note, gives the
following description of it : Rhodes
was one of the most magnificent
cities in the world, both from the
splendour of its buildings and pa-
laces, and the riches and opulence
of its inhabitants. Visited by the
commerce of all nations, it became
the emporium of that part of the
globe. In the interior part of the
city of Rhodes, there was no such
thing to be seen, as a large and small
house

house contiguous to each other.
The houses were all of the same
height, and of the same order of
architecture, so that the whole City
seemed to form but one building.
Its streets were very wide, and extended in length from one end of
the city to the other. So ingenious-
ly were they laid out, that they afforded on all sides the most elegant
and splendid appearance.

The walls particularly, whose extensive circumference was divided
by lofty and splendid towers, at regular distances, excited the admiration of all beholders. The elevated
tops of those towers, served for the
purpose of light houses to ships
making for the shore. Such indeed
was the magnificence of Rhodes,
that without seeing it, imagination
could

could form nothing equally pompous or splendid.

All the divisions of that great city being compared with the strictest regularity, constituted one whole, which was embellished by the walls, as a kind of crown.

This was the only city which might be said to be at the same time fortified against the attack of war, and ornamented as a palace.

The famous Colossus of Rhodes, which has been described by so many ancient writers, is said to have been overthrown by an earthquake.

The writings of Pliny and Strabo give us the best information respecting it.

The Rhodians were said to surpass the rest of the world in the
fine

fine arts, as well as in literature and science

They possessed the finest specimens of painting and of sculpture. The fertility of its territory, the mildness of its climate, but more than all its connection with almost all the countries of the globe, produced these advantages.

Rhodes was also said to be one of the most voluptuous, expensive, and dissipated cities in the world. The antients called it the City of Gallantry.

Conquered at last by the arms of the Emperor Vespasian, its fall was more rapid and tremendous from its anterior splendor and greatness. Its very situation as an island, which so long had been its principal safeguard and bulwark, became the

means

means of its utter downfall, and rendered a recovery impracticable.

The loss of liberty and the destruction of its disciplined forces, extinguished at once the flame of genius, which had produced so many wondrous specimens of art. Nations, their allies, who had so long held them in admiration, were pleased at the destruction of so powerful a neighbour. The unhappy, but feeble inhabitants of Rhodes, enervated as they were by luxury and riches, in vain looked up for foreign assistance in the day of trouble and adversity.

At length the long wished for order came for a preparation to move. On the morning of the 24th of February, the usual signal was made to sail.

Scarcely

Scarcely had the favorable breeze filled our sails, when our neighbours, the regiment de Rolle, accompanied us with their noble music.

Their vicinity, indeed, was always coveted by me, and on subsequent occasions, I have been still more gratified in an acquaintance with that regiment. At all times, when on duty with them, I have observed with delight their correct discipline and military deportment.

CHAP. IV.

Debarkation of the Troops under Major General Sir John Moore— Battle of the 13th of March— Battle of Alexandria—Death of Sir Ralph Abercrombie.

IT may be necessary here to observe, that in the brief details I have to give of this important and fortunate campaign, and of a country so classical and so interesting, I shall adopt the same manner in speaking of events in general terms, as in the description of North Holland, namely, to avoid as much as possible all invidious comparisons,

sons, as well as the mention of uncertain reports relative to individuals and regiments. Envy and evil
speaking, even in the private walk
of life, are sad and despicable pro-
pensities; but they have still a
more dangerous tendency when, in
a larger and more open field, they
attack the reputation of those employed in the service of their
country. Had I even my hands
full of truths, according to the charitable advice of Fontenelle, I would
not open them. In writing narratives, as well·as in conversation,
candour and forbearance are as indispensable as the Graces,

Senza de non ogni fatica e vana.

In speaking also of countries, it
is necessary to speak with caution.
To

To be surprised that men of other countries differ from us in their modes of dress, in their habits of living, and in general occupation, is surely unjust and disingenuous; we may as well be surprised that languages differ from each other.

I regret to have often observed too great a propensity amongst some of my countrymen to hold in a contemptuous and unworthy light, the conduct and actions of foreigners.

Prejudices and tastes always influence and sometimes determine those who have never resided in a foreign country, to consider all foreigners, even those conspicuous by their exploits and by their rank, a people of almost an inferior world.

Surely a want of consideration and reflection can alone afford such doc-

doctrine, or engender such unwar-
rantable ideas; yet it is well known
such ideas are daily exemplified.

I have met individuals of every
religion and every rank on the continent of Europe, in Asia and in
Africa, who, from their manners,
their conduct, and their education,
were in every way deserving the
name of superior and accomplished
men. The ridicule and prejudices
of all nations are softened and worn
off, by the familiar intercourse and
collision with each other.

In very few instances do we find
those who have not travelled, and
who have not associated with men
of other nations, entirely free from
prejudice, the result either of weakness of mind, and a want of knowledge of the world. Englishmen
in

in general are reproached with intolerance by foreigners, and of ar-
rogating a superiority over the rest
of mankind.

They are in consequence frequently ill received by them ; but,
on the other hand, when they evince
a conciliatory and forbearing conduct, when their manners and ad-
dress support and correspond with
the high military and naval character of the nation, which has
been so recently distinguished in
Europe, no people are more respected, or receive more politeness
and attention.

Let every one, therefore, who
proposes to travel into foreign countries, shake off all prejudice, all
pride, and every imaginary superiority ; assuring himself, that

amongst

amongst every people may be
found advantages, as well as dis-
advantages, the virtues as well as
the vices of mankind.

The fleet arrived and anchored
in the well-known bay of Aboukir
on the 1st of March; but a series
of boisterous and uncertain weather prevented the debarkation
until the morning of the 8th.

This unavoidable delay afforded
to the French army, commanded by
the General Menou, a great opportunity to defend himself, and to
establish a position close to the
shore, which was obvious to every
one would render the landing difficult and arduous.

Alacrity, great military talents,
and unbounded assiduity, the at-
tributes invariable in a French
army,

army, were not wanting on this occasion ; but it has been the opinion
of many that General Menou, in
this instance, was guilty of what
the great King of Prussia esta-
blishes as one of the first military
faults*; namely, that he despised,
or rather that he did not hold in
sufficient respect, the force and the
nature of the enemy opposed to
him. He omitted therefore, and
lost an opportunity, of which he
ought to have availed himself with
decision. In other words, he left
idle in Alexandria, a distance of
only of six leagues, several thousands of his troops. Had they
been at Aboukir, the chances were
at least precarious and doubtful,
and the victories in Egypt, a period
from which the English troops have

gained

gained a credit and character until then unknown, had never been.

From the date of that expedition, it is well known the English army have assumed a conduct and maintained a name in Europe, which places them in the highest estimation, even of the most powerful nations on the Continent, and has gained for them the esteem of their own Sovereign.

The greatest number of men which could be conveniently placed in the boats for the purpose of landing amounted to about five thousand.

The arrangement of the boats was very ably conducted by the naval officer on this occasion. On the near approach of the line of boats to the shore, a destructive and

and heavy fire opened from the whole of the enemy's entrenched position, and many officers and men were killed and wounded before they had reached the shore. The guns from the castle of Aboukir, in several instances, reached the right of the line of boats. As the troops made their first efforts to effect their debarkation, the fire of the enemy redoubled on every side. Several regiments formed rapidly, and pressed on with ardor to gain the ridge of the Sand Hills occupied by the enemy.

It was a moment of anxious doubt. On its success depended the character of the English army.

The attempts, as may easily be imagined, were bravely and skilfully resisted by the French troops, who

upon

upon this, and upon every other occasion, during the campaign, maintained their high military character.

A corps of the enemy's cavalry, hitherto unperceived, debouched from the rear of the Sand Hills, and wheeling rapidly, attacked the left of the troops before they had sufficiently formed. The shock of this charge was serious, and was repulsed only after some considerable time by the succession of reinforcements arriving from the boats. At midday, the enemy finding his efforts unavailing to resist the English troops, fell back about a league, and covering effectually the retreat of his rear-guard.

In the course of the day, nearly the whole of the troops landed. My regiment

regiment was ordered to invest the fort of Aboukir, and did not for some time afterwards leave that point.

The fortress of Aboukir at a distance has a respectable appearance. Against the Turks and Arabs it served as a place of security for the French troops, but it was not probable it would now long hold out, when regularly attacked. The ruins of the city of Aboukir are not very considerable, and scarcely any vestiges of its ancient splendour are to be found.

Near this spot was supposed to be the ancient castle of Canopus, or of Heraclea; and upon the left, about three leages distant, are still to be seen various ruins, probably those of Heraclea. Some of these

monu-

monuments have resisted alike the
ravages of time and of man, but
the present inhabitants in their
neighbourhood, are as ignorant of
either the origin or meaning of these
monuments of antiquity as though
they had never been.

The collected forces under the
immediate orders of Sir R. Abercrombie soon advanced to a vicinity of the French army, which had
now been considerably reinforced,
and were strongly posted on a line
of hills, near the ruins of the celebrated Alexandrian Library.

On the evening of the 12th,
orders were received for the greater
part of the troops at Aboukir to
move forthwith. These troops, reinforced by a battalion of marines,
marched immediately at sun-set.
After a long and very harassing
march

march during the night, impeded
as they were by a heavy and uncertain road, through a desert of
sand, they at length reached the
point of their destination.

The marines, though unaccustomed to long marches, bore up
with their usual firmness against the
fatigues of the march.

At midnight, I well remember the
welcome appearance of the range
of lights, discovering the position of
the English army. Beyond these,
with the intervening distance of
half a league, the more extended
line of the French, who had also
fires along the whole of their position.

Our repose here was of short continuance. At four in the morning,
the whole of the troops were again

under

under arms. The brigade, to which
my regiment was attached, formed
on this occasion the extreme left
of the army. After the space of
an hour, a heavy cannonade from
the French line, which in the first
instance was but feebly answered,
announced to us the commence-
ment of the engagement. I had
an opportunity of witnessing the
advance and attack of the cavalry
upon our right and center.

In the mean time, my regiment,
leading the brigade, received a
smart salutation from the enemy's
light artillery. We observed at the
line of hills a brigade of six guns,
supported by cavalry. These guns
occasioned us some loss, but they
did not think proper to relinquish
their strong commanding position;
and

and as the brigade advanced, they fell back, still keeping up a sharp fire.

A singular instance of the correct firing of the French artillery occurred here. A shot from the guns above mentioned grazed the officer who carried the colours, and killed two men. The brigade were advancing rapidly ; it was of course necessary to change the position of the guns ; notwithstanding which, six shots successively killed or wounded men in the same company, which were immediately following the colours.

On the right and center the battle soon took a favorable turn. The enemy abandoned about mid-day the line of hills.

I per-

I perceived the English descending into the plains, advancing in open columns, and taking the route to Alexandria. The left wing, in the mean time, kept parallel with the line of march, and approached the canal of Alexandria and lake Mareotis.

A point called the Green Hill, well known to the army in that country, was now occupied within range of the enemy's artillery. We suffered considerable loss here.

The French army having about three o'clock in the afternoon re-occupied their positions and batteries on the heights of Nicopolis, now turned upon their pursuers, and poured into the long extended line of the English a tremendous shower

shower of balls and grape-shot. My regiment lost twenty-seven men, without returning a single musket.

The very commanding position of the enemy, supported by the garrison of Alexandria, the considerable reinforcements he had received, and the rapid approach of evening, induced the Commander of the Forces to suspend all further attack. The brigades received orders to halt, and soon afterwards fell back.

At sun-set, the regiment filed into the space allotted for them in the second line in rear of the line of Sand Hills, held by the enemy the preceding evening.

The right and reserve of the army occupied the ruins of the Ptolomean palace or library, once so celebrated and distinguished. Several parts of the

the walls are still of considerable height and extent. Fragments of columns are found in the vicinity; and the shaking of the earth still indicates the destruction of great edifices buried beneath. Subterranean researches made near the spot might also ascertain the fate of those superb buildings in the time of the Ptolemies.

In no place, perhaps, are more striking and more accumulated examples of the varied industry, and stupendous labours of the ancient Egyptians to be found, than in the vicinity of Alexandria. Immediately beyond the ruins of the Palace, and closely bordering upon the sea, are the vestiges of baths, several apartments, of which still exist, and are ornamented with vaulted arches. These

These evince the magnificence and extent of the palace they once decorated.

An interval of seven days permitted both armies to make preparations for another battle. On this battle, in all probability, depended the fate of Egypt. The arrival of the French Commander in Chief, the General Menou in Alexandria, with the reinforcement of nine thousand men, occupied without doubt the consideration of the English Commander.

He was placed in an arduous, but conspicuous station, at a distance of more than one thousand leagues from his native country, and at the head of an army, which, if overthrown, must be lost without the escape of an individual, afforded him

him ample subject for reflection. The advantages of the enemy were manifold. An infantry, composed of excellent soldiers, who had traversed with Napoleon the plains of Italy, and on which they had ever been victorious. An artillery, numerous and admirably appointed, together with a cavalry of the first description, and mounted on Arabian horses. I have never seen in the army of any country superior men to those of the French cavalry in Egypt.

Ere the dawn of the 21st of March, the troops, under orders of Sir R. Abercrombie, were under arms. The earliest light announced to us the intention of the enemy. A demonstration upon the extreme left, upon the canal of Alexandria, a point

a point which could afford no material object to the enemy, was in
the first instance essayed ; but in
the space of a quarter of an hour,
the impetuous attack on all our
picquets, left no doubt as to his real
intention.

The right of the English army was
supported by a battery, and strong
redoubts, and occupied by a considerable body of troops. In rear of
this division were the ruins of the
palace before mentioned, the whole
of which were filled with troops. In
the rear of these also were the brigade, commanded by Sir John Stew-
art, forming the right of the second
line. The flank of all this force was
again supported by gun-boats, who
were enabled to enfilade the French
army on their approach to the English

lish line. These gun-boats were admirably served during the whole of the arduous day, and the manner in which they were managed reflects the highest credit on their commander.

The left of the French army vigorously attacked the position of the ruins, the whole of which had been embattled by the English, who defended them with excessive obstinacy.

After the attack had continued a short time, the English seemed to give way a little, and the French pushed forward.

The cavalry of the enemy at the same time advanced, and made a charge round the redoubt, some of whom endeavoured to force the points least defended. The regiment

ment stationed in this redoubt, the 28th, deserved the highest praise on this occasion.

The English, although hard pressed by this prodigious shock, made the most obstinate effort to maintain themselves.

The brigade, above mentioned, from the second lines, instantly advanced ; and, at the most fortunate moment, retrieved the loss of ground.

In the mean time, the centre of the French army, (from what cause is unknown), did not push to the utmost their forces in that quarter.

They seemed to refuse both their infantry and cavalry, and contented themselves with a violent and well supported cannonade. About this period Sir R. Abercrombie was carried

ried past the left of the regiment severely wounded.

Near eleven o'clock, the left wing of the French army began to shew symptoms of hesitation and inquietude. Several of their batteries were put into retreat. These were effectually preserved to them from our total want of cavalry. At length, after witnessing their ranks constantly thinned and impeded by heaps of wounded, the whole army gradually fell back, leaving on the field of battle a numerous dead. The French general of cavalry, Roizes, was killed in the charge near the redoubt in the early part of the morning. In the pocket of this officer was found the order of battle of General Menou, written on the preceding day, a copy of which is here-

hereafter inserted. This order plainly indicates what might have been expected by us, had Providence not on that day, favoured the cause of England.

CHAP.

CHAPTER V.

March to Rosetta—Fort St. Julian—
Rosetta—March of the Army—
Pyramids—Ramin or Desert Wind
—Mamelouks—Ruins of the City of
Memphis.

A VERY few days subsequent to
the victory of the 21st of March, a
strong body of troops, of which my
regiment formed a part, were detached to Rosetta, and of which the
French were then in possession.

The march of this detachment
was extremely laborious, and they
were subjected to many privations.
The

The weather, even at this early season of the year, began to be sultry and oppressive during the day. At night, as we were without camp equipage, the troops were constantly in the open air, and exposed to a heavy dew, and much cold.

This continual contrast, together with bad and precarious food, caused some unhealthiness; but, in the midst of a desert, such as between Alexandria and Rosetta, without any expectation of aid, and an enemy in our front, it was absolutely necessary to bear up against all trifling and imaginary indisposition.

On the third day, from leaving the line of Alexandria, we observed to our left a fort, which had been formerly constructed to defend the mouth of the Nile. At present

F

there

there is a considerable distance between the fort and the sea. The
enemy had now possession of this
station.

It is a square fortress, flanked
with thick towers at the angles, and
having batteries which are mounted
with heavy guns.

On the right of our line of march,
we observed the forests of date trees,
and also sycamore which surround
Rosetta, and which at a distance
give it a pleasing appearance.

Rosetta, called by the ancients
Raschid, stands on the Bolbitine
Branch of the Nile. Not far distant are the ruins of Bolbitinum,
where at this day is situated the
convent of Abu-mandor.—Rosetta
was formerly of much greater extent,

tent, as the ancient circumvallation, sufficiently demonstrates.

On the side of the Nile where Rosetta is built, scarcely any thing is to be seen but deserts and sands, with the exception of the gardens which surround the town, some of which are considerable, and possess many plantations. On the opposite bank, the delightful prospect of the Delta, and an island of about a league in length, very much improves the situation of the houses built near the Nile.

In the neighbourhood of Rosetta, I first witnessed the optical pheno- menon, called *mirage*, so common in Egypt. The traveller, when in the desert, overcome with fatigue and thirst which nothing will ap-

parently

parently allay, imagines that he sees
before him a vast lake.

The agreeable illusion for a time
fascinates ; but as he proceeds on
his way, disappointment and regret
as quickly succeed.

The mirage is produced by the
reflection of salient objects on the
oblique rays of the sun, refracted by
the heat of the burning soil and
sands.

It is impossible to give an adequate description of it.

At mid-day, when the sun has
obtained his meridian, its influence
has the greatest effect on the observer.

During the night, the mist and
fogs were extreme. My regiment
being employed in the reduction of
the

the fort above mentioned, an accident occurred, which I will here cite to corroborate this assertion.

Our batteries erected against the fortress were severely handled by the enemy.

We had very few men, about 500, to perform the duties which were incessant, and the necessity of closely watching the enemy to resist sorties, became in consequence imperious.

Being myself stationed in the battery at night, the subaltern officer was at some considerable distance in advance contiguous to the fort, with a small picquet. On visiting his sentries, he had given orders to them to fire, without previously chal lenging, on all who might approach them from the fort. Some alarm was suddenly given ; he had scarce-

ly

ly walked but a few yards from his station, when unfortunately missing his way, in consequence of the condensed mist, he returned in the direction from the fort, and was shot dead by his own sentry.

This young officer was much respected by his regiment.

The division at Rosetta was daily augmented by reinforcements from Alexandria; and shortly afterwards, the French troops having rapidly quitted their position in that vicinity, commenced its march in the direction of Demenhur.

It may be unnecessary to relate the various circumstances of this march towards Cairo, which shortly afterwards was given out to be the object of our destination. Scarcely any thing of consequence occurred
in

in this march, which was long, dilatory, and laborious.

The Fort of Ramaneigh alone occasioned some delay by its resistance.

Ramaneigh is a small fortified position upon the Nile; in the present instance, it was necessary to force it from the enemy, in order to allow of the transport of provisions and baggage in the boats; it would also be impossible to advance into the country and leave so considerable a body of French troops in the rear of the army. The French General La Grange who had previously commanded at Rosetta, having thrown a body of three hundred infantry into the fort, occupied with the remainder of his division the dyke in front of Ramaneigh, in

E 4   which

which he placed the whole of his artillery, and supported his left with a considerable body of cavalry.

The English army marched at midnight previous to their arrival before Ramaneigh, and about ten in the morning halted within sight of the French position. This march was extremely laborious. We passed over several leagues of sand, many fields of tobacco, and others filled with melons, with which the soldiers gladly refreshed themselves.

An hour after mid-day the army was again in motion. On the approach of the advanced guard, the French voltigeurs and two pieces of flying artillery endeavoured to arrest its progress. A brigade of English skirted the Bank of the Nile, and in conjunction with the gun-

gun-boats maintained a brisk fire upon the fort. The enemy was unwilling to permit the exertions of the English General to be thus concentrated. He therefore moved to his left, covering with the cavalry the whole of his left flank, and demonstrated an intention of attacking two brigades of the English, who composed our right wing, and were without cavalry. These troops were accordingly formed in expectation of the attack of the cavalry, who appeared to be in number about four complete squadrons.

The whole line of the French were at a brisk trot; already the shots from the riflemen on the enemy's flanks flew around us, and the trumpets had sounded a charge. When at about a hundred paces distant, they

f 5   rapidly

rapidly wheeled to the right and
left, and defiled again to the rear,
unmasking at the same eight pieces
of flying artillery, who immediately
cannonaded our squares. Not a
moment was to be lost; each regiment instantly deploying, returned
the fire, and obliged the artillery to
retire, after sustaining on both sides
some loss.

The French General and his staff,
admirably mounted, were distinctly
seen manoeuvring the cavalry. We
were much astonished on the following morning to find the enemy
had retired during the night, and
abandoned the position of Ramaneigh.

The troops were sadly troubled
here with insects and reptiles of various descriptions.

The

The army bivouacked in rear of the dyke. Worn out with a march of fixteen hours, and the subsequent engagement, the soldiers were no sooner upon the ground than they fell asleep, regardless of the heavy dew, the various animals above mentioned, crawling around them, and even the want of food. Three men of the regiment were bitten by scorpions, and were rendered incapable of serving in the ranks for some considerable time afterwards. In the day, the musquitoes and flies were almost insufferable, and at every meal it was not uncommon for the dish placed before us to be totally covered with flies, which no exertion could destroy or drive away. It was usual in all marches, for every officer and

soldier

soldier to carry over his shoulder a canteen containing about three pints of water.

After the march, the first thing required, was to hang up the alcarass, a jar filled with water, to cool in the current of air ; the porous nature of, the alcarass renders the water cool and refreshing, and they may be found in every house, as the Egyptians consider them indispensable.. An unquenchable and burning thirst continually demanded water. Who indeed, who has not suffered in such a climate, experienced similar privations, and waded through the sands of Egypt, can form an adequate idea of the pains of extreme thirst ? The whole Nile seemed inadequate to our desires. As he finished his daily march,

march, the unwary soldier rushed to the welcome bank of the river, and plunging into the stream, there found his death from the fatal effects of the excess of drinking water.

The army remained some time at Amm-el-Dinar. Here the heat of the weather became excessive. The fatigue of the marches unbounded, and the pains of thirst insupportable.

The unhappy soldiers were seen rolling in the sand, and giving themselves up without hope, whilst the sun darted upon them its vertical and fiery rays.

Times and circumstances were no respecters of persons. Every officer was equally exposed. The greater part of them carried their baggage, if such it might be called in a knapsack slung over the shoulder; and

and on the arrival at the position for the night, lay down, if not employed on duty in the sands or fields : in common with many others, I myself shared without intermission this lot, from the 8th of March, the day of our landing, until the occupation of Alexandria in the September following; during the whole of this period, I never experienced the least diminution of health.

The dreadful southerly wind, called by the Egyptians the kamsin, or wind of fifty days, commenced at this period its fatal career.

They prevail generally in the fifty days preceding and following the equinox. They are the winds of the desert, and are justly called poisonous, from the baneful effects they occasion to the human frame.

It

It is difficult to form an idea of
its excessive heat, or to calculate
·upon its destructive tendency. Af-
·ter a day spent under the burning
rays of the sun, and worn down
with a long and toilsome march, the
wearied soldier expected some little
repose at the approach of evening.

It was in vain that he cherished
this pleasing hope. Instead of cool
and refreshing breezes, the deadly
blast of the kamsin assailed him,
·and prevented the necessary repose.
It may be said to resemble the confined air of an oven. It produces
a change on all animated bodies,
affects immediately the lungs, and
causes pain.

The skin also becomes parched
and dry: no quantity of water
drank by the unhappy sufferer produces

duces perspiration, and it is in vain
to seek for coolness.

The atmosphere assumes a dreadful aspect, and the sun no longer
appears.

Notwithstanding its absence, even
stone, iron, and other inanimate
bodies become hot.

The poor Arabs were seen terri-
fied, and running about in groupes,
throwing themselves into the Nile,
where they remain for many hours;
others shut themselves up in their
houses, and dug pits in the earth.

If the traveller in the desert should
be overtaken with one of the squalls
of wind which sometimes happen,
a suffocation and sudden death are
inevitable.

Even the camels and horses have
a mode to resist this horrible enemy,
by

by putting the nose into the sand during the squall; nature has pointed out to them the necessity of thus defending themselves.

Let us suppose for a moment, the contrast of our own climate, of which so many complain, to this afflicted country.

Let us calculate on the numberless privations and inconveniences to which the people of Egypt are exposed, and compare them to the advantages of the more fortunate Europe. Ought not such a reflection cause us to feel grateful for the enjoyment of so many blessings.

The kamsin is more or less felt in the island of Cyprus, and of Rhodes, but passing as it does over a considerable portion of the Mediterranean, its violence is somewhat alleviated

viated by the coolness of the waters.
I have experienced it in Minorca,
and in Gibraltar: in the latter place,
it is generally called an easterly wind
or levanter : it is extremely oppressive on that rock; and during its
continuance, totally changes the
nature of the climate.

When the winds proceed alone
from the Deserts of Arabia and
Lybia, their force is at its extreme
height. The air which cover these
immense plains, meeting with neither lakes, rivulets, nor water of any
description, but always scorched by
the rays of a burning sun, and the
reflexion of the sand, becomes naturally more arid and destructive.
This naturally accounts for its insupportable power in the latitude
in which we then were; namely, so
very

very contiguous to the deserts above mentioned.

The heat of the weather in Egypt so great during the day, is succeeded at night by extremely heavy dews. After sun-set, clothes exposed to the air are soaked through, and wet, as if with rain : these dews are more or less copious, according to the prevailing wind ; during the kamsin, they are not so heavy. On our marches, we frequently passed through fields of tobacco, and others of considerable extent, filled with melons and cucumbers. The leaves of them, notwithstanding the aridity of the soil, are fresh and green. This denotes the reviving nature of the dew, and its effect upon vegetation.

The army, continuing its march, arrived at Embabey. Beyond this desolate

solate place is a rising ground, which at a little distance is flanked by a wood of date and citron trees, the largest I had seen in Egypt. On this precise spot Napoleon attacked the army of the Mamelouks, who were here resolved to dispute his passage to Cairo. On the evening preceding this battle, the French divisions arrived and encamped in succession, the position being marked out by Napoleon in person.

The Mamelouks, who had thrown up entrenchments, the vestiges of which are still seen, having early in the morning under Murad-Bey in person reconnoitred the French position, resolved to attack them forthwith. Confident and impetuous, and holding as they usually do in contempt all species of infantry,

fantry, they commenced a furious
attack on one of the French divisions. It was here that Napoleon
is reported to have said to his army,
—" Push on, and recollect that
from the summit of those monuments, forty centuries watch over
us."

This division, by a continued and
well-supported fire, resisted and
stopped the efforts of the enemy.
It was in vain that the brave and
hardy Mamelouks essayed a second
charge. The rapid glance of Napoleon had, by a manœuvre equally
rapid, exposed them to a cross fire
from other divisions, and thereby
commenced their discomfiture.—
The numerous riflemen of the
French dreadfully assailed them.
Worn out at length by continual
loss,

loss, and separated from each other
from want of sufficient military
skill, a part of them took the road
to the deserts, whilst another part
fled towards Cairo in the utmost
disorder. From this spot also we
first were gratified and astonished
at the distant view of the pyramids
of Egypt. The sensation felt on
resting the eye for the first time on
these stupendous monuments it is
impossible to describe. Let any
one imagine that he is beholding
objects, whose origin and whose
founder is unknown even to the
most remote historian, monuments
that have been beheld by the
greatest heroes, and monarchs of
antiquity, and that have equally
resisted the attacks of destructive
time, and more destructive man.

It

It is impossible to see and approach them without a mixture of awe and of satisfaction. Few men now in existence can ever behold them. The difficulties and dangers attending a traveller in that country were always great, and in future will be still greater.

It would be impracticable for an individual, of whatever rank or fortune, in these days to traverse Egypt. An escort, amounting almost to an army, would be indispensable; and even then he must watch against the treachery of his own guard.

When the English army were there, a friendly understanding with the people of the country, and an alliance with the Turks and Mamelouks afforded security, and even
leisure,

leisure, to make observation upon the customs, manners, and state of this interesting country. Although now desolate and fallen for ages into decay, the recollection of former splendour and its classical history, must ever render it an object of importance, and worthy of the deepest research.

At this period the corps of Mamelouks, under the command of Osman Bey, joined us.

This force was of the highest importance at such a crisis, our own cavalry being but weak in number. The Mamelouks made a fine appearance. We admired the appearance of their noble horses, their rich and sumptuous appointments, and the wonderful rapidity of their movements.

At

At the time of the invasion of
the French army into Upper Egypt,
they were always sufficiently skill-
ful to avoid their pursuers. Accustomed to scour the deserts, to
live precariously, and to disregard
the burning rays of the sun, they
possessed advantages over the French
army, who could but seldom come
up with them.

Ibrahim and Murad Bey, the
chiefs of the Mamelouks, have
usually under their command about
2000 men. There are also many inferior Beys, who have troops under
them, and who usually combine together on any urgent demand for
their services.

These men, forming the military
power of Egypt, send detachments
into the different towns and villages

G   through

through the country, in order to maintain the authority of their corps, collect tributes, and improve every opportunity of extortion.

Their despotism and tyranny were so dreaded by the Egyptians, that, in the first instance, they hailed the advance of the French army, and were happy at the defeat of the Mamelouks.

The French army found in them their most formidable enemy. They are generally brave, or rather ferocious; but at the same time they are an inconstant and interested character, and little faith or reliance can be placed in them. The Beys were naturally well disposed to join the English, by whose alliance they hoped to drive away the French troops, and to recover the country they

they had lost. To suppose them
friends to the English from any other
cause, is to reckon too largely; and
to think as we often do in England,
namely, that we possess more friends
than we really have.

The army continued to advance
towards Grand Cairo. The garrison
there was commanded by the
French General Belliard, and a-
mounted to about 9000 effective
men, protected by batteries, and an
entrenched camp. In the midst of
the month of July, we were encamped within three leagues of the pyramids, the right wing stretching towards the Desert, and the left upon
the Nile. In front of this army were
a considerable division of the Turkish army, and the whole of the Mamelouks. Scarcely a morning pass-

ed

ed that we did not witness a skir-
mish or single combat between these
last, and some of the French Vi-
dettes

In traversing the plains between
the city of Cairo, and the pyramids
of Gizah, the impressions of history
and poetry are retraced in the memory; and the extraordinary situations in which they are recalled, sof-
ten down the fatigues experienced
in so sultry a journey.

The road, or rather tract, is chiefly through sands, and at occasional
distances are several villages. At a
distance of two leagues is one superior to the rest, situated on the
edge of the desert, and surrounded
by the lime and orange trees: the eye
reposes on these verdant objects with
delight. We are consoled for the prospect

pect of the Desert, which stretches itself before us in boundless immensity, and presents gloomy ideas to all who behold it.

Arrived at the celebrated pyramids, of which so much has been said and reported by various travellers, our party sat down and reposed themselves at the base of these extraordinary monuments of antiquity.

In countries distant from this, the mind in general is so familiar with external objects, that we scarcely notice or perceive their existence, and they very rarely excite a new emotion, but the astonishment which the contemplation of the pyramids is calculated to produce, is suddenly called forth at the sight of these prodigies.

They

They have withstood the lapse of ages, which together with the hands of man, have had but little effect against them.

The solidity of their construction, and their extraordinary dimensions have secured them against every attempt, and seem to promise to them an everlasting duration.

To the Egyptians they are at once their boast, and their country derives celebrity from them as the monuments and work of the extraordinary labours of their ancestors.

In another point of view, circumstances render this singular part of the country by no means desirable. To the south, a long and frightful void presents nothing which can animate the parched and weary sight: Nothing but barren and scorched

scorched sand, over which passes
the sirocco wind, the enemy of every
living animal.

> Ne gregi, ni armenti
> Guida, bifolco mai, guida pastore.

The excessive heat experienced
in those regions surpasses all description; and to endeavour to speak
fully of its effects, would pass but
for a traveller's story. On the very
day of our visit to the Pyramids, several soldiers died from its effects.
Life indeed here is almost insupportable, were it not buoyed up by
collateral circumstances. We are
surrounded by monuments of history. The recollection is encou-
raging, that we tread upon the
classic ground of the Cæsars and of
the Ptolomies; a permission, which

nothing

nothing but the combined events of the war in Egypt could possibly grant or secure to us.

Not far from the Pyramids are still to be seen and traced the ruins of Memphis.

We arrived at and crossed with difficulty the remains of an extensive bridge of many arches. One traces nothing very remarkable in the ruins of the city. Ages have rolled over them, and left nothing but confused and indescribable masses of stone and rubbish.

At the extremity of the city, towards the Nile, appeared the remains of a palace. Here were observable some pillars laying in the dust, on which were inscribed the names of Egypt, India, and Asia.

Although the ruins of Memphis do not contain so many monuments uninjured

uninjured by time, comparatively,
with many others of the celebrated
cities of Egypt, yet they cover a
large space of ground, and give high
ideas of its former splendour and
magnificence. Its antiquity is extremely remote. Some few of its
vestiges of grandeur still exist. We
took notice of the city gates, some
small parts of which still remain,
built of a large species of bricks,
that had formerly been faced with
hewn stone. This last has now fallen down, both from the interior
and the sides; yet the gate is still
standing, and may continue to stand
for many years. It is of very considerable thickness, and, in former
days, must have been of immense
size and heighth. Its antiquity is

sup-

supposed to be of the period of the
first Ptolomies.

We observed here also a large
space of ground, in the form of a
square. Many ruins in Egypt wear
a similar aspect ; remarkable from
a double row of pedestals, surrounding the sides of that square. The
lower part of these pedestals are
sunk in the ground. Their capitals
are strewed in confusion around.

The French author, Denon, whose
writings on Egypt are unequalled,
thus describes the vicinity of Bene-
suef, in upper Egypt, where numerous ruins still exist. " Some vestiges of villages, overwhelmed by
the sand, may be discovered ; and
they present the afflicting sight of
daily devastation, produced by the

con-

continual encroachment of the de-
sart on the soil, inundated with
sand.

" Nothing is so melancholy to the
feelings, as to march over these
ruined villages, to tread under foot
the roofs of the houses, and the tops
of the minarets ; and to think that
these were once cultivated fields,
flourishing trees, and the habitations of man. Every thing living
has disappeared. Silence is within,
and around every wall; and the
deserted villages are like the dead,
whose skeletons strike with terror."

In another part, speaking of the
considerable relics of Hermopolis:

" I saw, at length, the porticoes
of Hermopolis ; the huge masses of
the ruins of which, gave me the
earliest idea of the splendour, which
cha-

characterizes the colossal architecture of the Egyptians.

"On each of the blocks, of which this edifice was composed, I fancied that I saw the words—Posterity, Eternity."

In all probability, if the ground contiguous should be dug up, a number of statues and valuable curiosities might be discovered. Here and there are heaps of broken pillars, and columns of marble and granite, with their shafts half sunk in the ground. Such is the fate of the once magnificent cities of the world. They are the work of man, and they perish like himself. Thebes, Memphis, Alexandria, which were once the glory and terror of the earth, are now no more.

Although

Although I have said little of
Egypt, and have merely briefly stat-
ed a few of the military movements;
yet, it is not to be supposed, that
in the most sultry latitude of the
Pyramids, and under a burning sun,
rendered still more intense by hot
and inflammatory winds, such movements could take place without
unceasing labour, without fatigue,
and accumulated trouble to the
army. The remembrance of these
deserts still affords a pleasing subject
of retrospection, but it is nevertheless a recollection of respect; and
now that I breathe the moderate
climate of Europe, I forget not that
I have trodden the land of Egypt.

The fatigues of the troops in general were very great, and their privations greater. From the moment
of

of quitting the lines of Alexandria
we acted in presence of an enemy.
Every morning, so early as two
hours after midnight, the noise of
dromedaries and camel drivers' announced to us the hour of march.

This was not only for one or a
few mornings, but continued more
or less during the months of May,
June, July, and August.

After the daily march, which generally lasted until mid-day, we reposed, if the baggage had arrived,
under a single piece of thin can-
vass.

The usual food, consisted of a portion of salt meat from the shipping,
sometimes a ration of buffaloe, and
biscuit from the Turks of the most
vile description ; occasionally, also,
a small quantity of spirits. Officers
and

and soldiers all fared alike. All
however did not support themselves
alike against existing circumstances.
The health of the troops, in consequence of this continued exposure
to the climate, precarious and bad
food, but more than all from the
baneful force of disorders, [incident
to the country, visibly began to decline.

They had successively to combat
with the dysentery, its consequent
debility, and the still more terrible
ophthalmia. When ill, and laying
upon the sand, they were tormented
by innumerable flies, scorpions, ta-
rantulas, and other poisonous insects.
The army, in a word, were in a
feeble state. Fortunately the arrival of the troops from India, which
had debarked at Suez, supplied our
ranks.

ranks. Without them, the task of subduing Cairo must have been arduous, if not impracticable. The division of the army before Cairo was certainly fearfully diminished.

Savary, Sonnini, and Volney have spoken sometimes in raptures of this land of Egypt. One would imagine it to be a terrestrial paradise. To me, it appeared like its once celebrated cities—a country which had long been buried.

Let us see by the following letters, what the individuals of the French army thought of this country.

FRENCH LETTER.

TRANSLATION.—LETTER I.

Boulac near Cairo, July 27th.

To the General:

We are arrived at length, my friend,

friend, at the spot so much, and so
eagerly desired ! How different is it
from what the most cool and temperate imagination had figured it to
be ! This execrable city is inhabited
by a set of wretches, who sit all day
before their filthy huts, smoking, and
taking coffee, or eating pumpions,
and drinking water. It is easy
enough to lose one's self for a whole
day in the abominable and narrow
streets of this illustrious capital.

The quarter of the Mameloucs is
the only one which is habitable.
The Commander in Chief resides
there in a tolerable handsome house,
which belonged to one of the Beys.

I have written to the Chief of
Brigade, Dupuis, at present General
and Governor of Cairo, to reserve
a house

a house for you. I have not yet received an answer.

The division is quartered in a kind of town, called Boulac, upon the Nile, about half a league from Cairo. We are all lodged in houses deserted by their owners ; and wretched enough in all conscience.

General Lannes has just received an order to take the command of Menou's division, in the room of Vial, who is going to Damietta, with a battalion. He assures me that he will not accept it. The light battalion, and general Verdier, are are stationed near the Pyramids, on the left bank of the Nile, till the position which he occupies can be fortified, so as to receive a garrison of an hundred men.

A bridge

A bridge is intended to be thrown
over the river, nearly opposite Djiza.
The spot is at present occupied by
the reserve of the artillery and engineers. Regnier's division is stationed two or three leagues in front
of Cairo.

You have not an idea of the fa-
tiguing marches we made to get to
Cairo, never halting till three or
four o'clock in the afternoon, after
broiling in the sun all day; the
greatest part of the horse without
food : obliged to glean whatever the
division which preceded us, had
left us in these detestable villages,
which they had frequently pillaged :
and harassed during the whole
march by those bands of robbers
called Bedouins, who killed not only

our

our men, but our officers, at five and six paces from the main body.

We had an engagement the day we arrived in the neighbourhood of Cairo.

The Mamelouks, who had the good sense to place themselves on the left bank of the Nile, offered us battle, and were defeated.

We call it the battle of the Pyramids. They lost, to speak without exaggeration, a thousand men ; and of these, a great number perished in attempting to cross the Nile.

The troops are neither paid or fed. It is in fact, a land of desolation and horror, and we have reason to curse the day that witnessed our landing in this miserable country.

FRENCH

FRENCH LETTER.

TRANSLATION.—LETTER II.

Extract.

" Having organized a government at Alexandria, and secured a communication with the rest of the army, Buonaparte ordered every man to provide himself with five days provision, and made preparation for passing a desert of twenty leagues in extent, in order to arrive at the mouth of the Nile, and ascend that celebrated stream to Grand Cairo ; the principal object of the expedition.

We began our march on the fifth of July, and reached the river in a few days, fallingin on our route, with some detached parties of Mamelouks, who retired as we advanced.

It

It was not till the 12th that Buonaparte learned the Beys were marching to meet him with their united forces, and that he might expect to be attacked the next day.

He marched therefore, in order of battle, and took the necessary precautions.

General Buonaparte sent me forward to give the necessary intelligence with three armed sloops : with this little flotilla, I advanced about three leagues in front of the army, and came to anchor for the night opposite a village called Chebriki, where the Mamelouks were collected in force, and where the first action took place. I sent off my dispatches to the Commander in Chief that night : in these I gave him all the information I had been

able

able to obtain respecting the Mamelouks.

In the mean time the Mamelouks
were advancing upon our army.
They rode round and round it without finding any point where an impression might be made, and indeed
without any attempt at it. I presume that astonished at the manner
in which our army was drawn up,
they were induced to put off to a
future day, the decision of their
fortune and their empire. This af-
fair was trifling enough in itself;
the Mamelouks only lost about
twenty men, but we reaped a considerable advantage from it, that of
having given an extraordinary idea
of our tactics to an enemy unac-
quainted with any; who knows of
no other superiority in arms, than
that

that of strength and agility : without order and firmness, unable even to march in platoons, advancing in confused groups, and falling upon the enemy in sudden starts of wild and savage fury.

After the retreat of the Mamelouks, we advanced upon Cairo, where the decisive action took place. It was, in fine, on the 22d of July, that the army found itself at daybreak about three leagues from Cairo, and five from the so much celebrated pyramids. Here the Mamelouks, commanded by the famous Mourad, the most powerful of the Beys, awaited us : till three in the afternoon, the day was wasted in skirmishes : at length the hour arrived : our army flanked on the right by the Pyramids, and on the left

left by the Nile, perceived the enemy was making a movement : two
thousand advanced against our right :
never have I seen so furious a charge ;
giving their horses the reins, they
rushed on the divisions like a torrent,
and pushed in between them ; our
soldiers firm and immovable, allowed them to come within ten paces;
and then began a running fire, accompanied by some discharges of
artillery ; numbers of them fell, and
the rest immediately retired. They
returned, however, to the charge,
and were received in the same manner. Wearied out at length by our
resistance, they turned, and attacked
our left wing, to see if fortune would
there be more favourable to them.

The success of our right encourag-
ed Buonaparte. The Mamelouks had
thrown

thrown up a hasty entrenchment in
the village of Embabet, on the left
bank of the Nile, in which they had
placed thirty pieces of cannon, with
their attendants, and a small number of janissaries to defend the ap-
proaches : at the instant our soldiers
were rapidly advancing towards it,
six hundred Mamelouks sallied forth
from the works, surrounded our platoons, and endeavoured to cut them
down ; instead of succeeding, they
met their own deaths. Three hundred of them dropt on the spot, and
the rest, in their attempt to escape,
threw themselves into the Nile,
where they all perished. Despairing
now of any success, the main body
of the Mamelouks fled on all sides ;
set fire to their fleet, which soon
after blew up, and abandoned their
camp

camp to us, with more than four hundred camels, laden with baggage. Thus ended the day to the confusion of an enemy, who were possessed with the belief that they should cut us in pieces, and whose chief had boasted that he would cut off the heads of a thousand Frenchmen like gourds.

The army marched on that night to Gizah, the residence of Mourad, the chief of the Mamelouks.

The next day we crossed the Nile in flat-bottomed boats, and entered Cairo without resistance.

Here ends the narrative of our military operations. I propose now to give you some account of the miseries we underwent on our march, together with a brief description of the country we have traversed, and of the inhabitants.

Let us return to Alexandria. This city has nothing of its antiquity but its name. If there be any other relics of it, they remain utterly unregarded and unknown among a people, who appear to be scarce conscious of their own existence.

Leaving this city to ascend the Nile, you cross a desert, where every three or four leagues is found a well of brackish water.

Imagine to yourself the situation of an army obliged to pass these arid deserts, which do not afford the slightest shelter against the intolerable heat which prevails there. The soldier loaded with provisions, finds himself, before he has marched an hour, overcome by the heat, and

the

the weight of what he carries, and
throws away every thing that adds
to his fatigue, without thinking of
to-morrow. Thirst attacks him!
he has not a drop of water! Hunger—he has not a bit of bread!
It was thus, that amidst the horrors
which this faithful picture presents,
we beheld several soldiers die of
thirst, of hunger, and of heat; others,
seeing the sufferings of their com-
rades, blew out their brains; others
threw themselves into the Nile loaded as they were, and perished in
the water.

Every day of our march renewed
these dreadful scenes, and what was
never heard of before, what will
stagger all belief, the army, during
a march of seventeen days, never
tasted bread. The soldiers lived the
H 3   whole

whole of this time on gourds, melons, poultry, and such vegetables
as they found on their route. Such
was the food of all from the General to the private soldier. Even
the General Buonaparte was obliged
to fast often for eighteen or twenty
hours, because the privates, usually
arriving first, plundered the villages
of every article of subsistence, and
frequently reduced him to the necessity of satisfying himself with the
refuse of their hunger.

It is useless to speak of our drink.
We all live here under the law of
Mahomet, which forbids the use of
wine.

The country through which we
passed was uninteresting. The villages are crowded together. Their
construction is execrable, being
little

little more than heaps of mud trodden into some consistency, hollowed
out within. The husbandmen are
very laborious, and live on little,
but in a state of filth and degrada-
tion which excites horror.

Such is this Egypt, so celebrated
by travellers and historians.

LETTER III.

Au Caire Le 29 Thermidor an 6.

Je saisis avec empressement, mon
cher ami, l'occasion qui me procure
un de nos chefs d'escadron qui se
retire par demission, pour te faire
parvenir cette Lettre, dans l'espoir
qu'elle sera plus heureuse que cette
que je t'ai ecrite d'Alexandrie. La
Fregate qui en etoit porteur avant,

dit

dit on, été prise par les Anglois. Tu as sans doute appris, qu'après une navigation assez heureuse, nous nous étions emparès de l'isle de Malthe, et que de là nous avions fait voile pour l'Egypte,—nous sommes en effet arrivès devant Alexandrie le 14 Thermidor, et nous nous en sommes également emparès après une légère resistance.

Je ne saurois t'exprimer, mon cher ami, l'étonnement que j'ai éprouvée, en entrant dans cette ville, jadis si célèbre, dont il ne reste pas le moindre splendeur, et ou on ne trouve plus que les vestiges de quelques anciens Monumens, tels que la Colonne de Pompée, les Bains de Cléopatre, &c. L'Alexandrie moderne n'est plus qu'un Mas de Baraques de terre, formant des petites

Rues

Rues fort étroites, d'un mal propreté
au dessus de tout ce qu'on peut
imaginer, ce qui joint à la Chaleur
excessive de ce climat, fait qu'on
y respire un très mauvais air, qui
y'amène chaque année la peste.

A peine commençoit elle à cesser
ces ravages, loisque nous avons
abordé : plusieurs Batimens en
étoient encore infestés dans le port,
et j'ai encore vû porter en terre des
êtres vivants qui en étoient at-
tacqués. Je t'avoue que ce spectacle joint à l'air stupide et farouche
des Habitans du pays, m'a navré le
cœur—Je me suis demandé à moi-
même comment le Gouvernement
Françóis avoit fait tant d'efforts, et
exposé une armée de quarante mille
hommes, pour venir soumettre un
peuple si féroce, et si abrutté.

Telle

Telle est, mon cher ami, la question que je me suis faite en mettant le pied sur ce Sol brûlant, qui ne présente de tous parts que des Desserts immenses, entièrement depourvus d'eau, dans l'espace de quatorze Lieues, que nous avons traversées en partant d'Alexandrie.

Apres cette cruelle traversée, où les troupes ont beaucoup souffert de la Chaleur et de la soif, nous nous sommes approchés du Nil, dont les Rives sont un peu plus fecondes, mais toujours habitées par un peuple également farouches. Pendant nos trois premières Journées de Marche, nous avons continuellement été suivis par des Arabes, ou des Bedouins, qui sont des Brigands à cheval, accoutumès de vivre de pillage, et qui égorgeoient ceux qui,

qui, epuisès de soif et de fatigues, ne pourroient suivre la colonne.

Nous avons enfin rencontré les Mamelouks, qui sont les troupes que les Beys, au nombre de vingt-quatre qui gouvernent l'Egypte sous leur domination, tirent de Circassie et de Georgie, et tiennent à leur solde—Ces troupes sont toutes montées sur d'excellens chevaux Arabes : Elles ont voulus nous charger, mais le feu de la mous-quetterie, et du canon les ont bien-tot dispersés et fait retirer jusque sous les murs de Caire ou nous som-mes entré le 3 Thermidor après avoir complettement battu l'ennemi.

Je croyois en arrivant dans cette ville si célèbre par son commerce avec l'Inde, que nous y trouverions de tout en abondance, et un peuple

plus

plus civilisé, mais mon attente a été trompée, et à l'exception des Européens qui y sont établis, le peuple est aussi barbare, et aussi ignorant qu'à Alexandrie—D'après le léger apperçu que je te donne de l'Egypte, tu peus croire que l'armée n'est point contente de cette Expédition dans un pays dont les mœurs, la nouriture, et la chaleur, ne s'accomodent nullement avec notre manière de vivre en Europe—la majeure partie de l'armée est attaquée de la dysenterie, et quoique victorieuse, finira par y périr misérablement, si notre Gouvernement persiste dans ces projets ambitieux—Beaucoup d'officiers donnent leur demission, et je l'avoue que je la donnerois également, si j'avois espoir de trouver quelque emplois en France,

France ; mais denué de ressources, il faut prendre patience, et attendre que les évènemens apportent quelque changement dans la position critique on nous nous trouvons.

Nous ne savons si notre séjour sera long tems dans ces nouvelles Contrées, et si nous porterons plus loin nos conquêtes ; mais il paroit qu'on est disposé à garder le pays, car on y a déja organisé des municipalités—Une partie de l'armée est à la poursuite des Mamelouks, et je crois qu'on fera tous les efforts imaginables pour les atteindre avant qu'ils se soient retirés dans la Syrie, puis qu'ils se sont emparès de la caravane des Indes, qu'ils amenent avec eux, et qui est un objet très précieux.

Adieu, cher ami, donne moi de

8   tes

tes nouvelles dont je n'ai point reçu depuis celles que je reçus à Genoa.

Crois moi
ton sincère ami.

LETTER IV.

Au Caire, le 27 Thermidor.

Je n'ai reçu aucune Lettre de vous, depuis mon départ de Toulon, mon cher Général, et je crains bien que vous n'aviez reçu de moi aucune nouvelle. Je juge de vos inquiétudes à mon égard, par les bienfaits dont vous m'avez comblé ; jugez de la mienne par la reconnoissance qu'ils me commandent.

Cette lettre vous parviendra peut-être ; un de mes camarades la porte, et s'embarquera sur un neutre, d'ailleurs d'ailleurs les Anglois vainqueurs, sont cependant assez maltraités pour ne pouvoir tenir la mer, et laisseront j'espère pour quelque tems nos communications libres.

Avec quelle ardeur nous le désirons ! Depuis quatre mois nous ignorons et que sont devenus nos parens et amis. Nous avions laissé la republique entourée de factions, et à peine quelques gazettes insignificantes nous sont-elles parvenus. Tous les couriers ont été saisi : présage bien sinistre : le seul convoi qui portoit Tallien a été respecté.

Si les dépêches du Général sont parvenus, vous aurez appris que suis blessé, quoique au premier coup-d'œil ma blessure es assez légère. La Balle a respectée la langue, le gosier, les vaisseaux sanguins et la
machoire

machoire gauche. La playe va à merveille, je puis parler, et j'espère dans quinze jours manger autre chose que de la bouillie, ou plutot manger, car depuis un moi, je ne sais qu'avaler.

Je resterai ici, neanmoins ; mon soif sera hé à celui de l'armée, quoique j'y serve avec peu, et bien peu d'agrément, et quoique je suis bien sur qu'on ne me saura nul gré de ce sacrifice.

La campagne que nous venons de faire est sans contredit la plus penible qu'aient jamais fait les François. Nos marches forcées dans le desert sous un ciel brulant, sur un sable plus brulant encore, notre disette d'eau pendant cinque jours, de pain, pendant quinze,

quinze, de vin pendant trois mois, sans cesse au bivouac, exposée à une Rosée perfide qui aveugloit les imprudents—tout cela est bien plus terrible que les battailles et les sièges.

Il ne faut que de l'élan pour celles-ci, il faut pour l'autre du vrai courage, du courage de tête et d'ame.

Nous n'avons eu que deux battailles, et trois ou quatre combats : ou plutot nous n'avons eu que deux boucheries.

Les Mamelouks n'avoient que de la bravoure ; nous etions instruits et disciplinés.

Ils sont venu se briser sur nós battaillons quarrés, leur imprudente valeur les a fait se precipiter entre deux de ces masses redoutables,

doutables, et ils y ont trouvè leur tombe.

Vaincus, et sans autre espoir que de se sauver, ils fuyent avec leur ba-gage—ils ne sont plus à craindre—la constance du courage ne sauroit être l'apanage de l'ignorance, elle n'en posséde que l'léan.

D'ailleurs quelques forts élevées à l'entrèe du desert, et aux debouches de la Syrie, nous garrantissent d'eux ; et ensuite ou peut se re-cruter ce ramas d'esclaves ?

Les Arabes, Bedouins, et les ha-bitans sont aujourdhui nos seuls ennemis—les premiers sont inde-structibles. Voleurs par profession, et par institution reçue de race en race, il seroit plus difficile de les ci-viliser que de nous rendre sau-vages.

Les

Les liens de la societè leur se-
roient plus pénibles que les fatigues de cette vie affreuse, que
l'habitude et l'ignorance les em-
pêchent de trouver horrible. On
ne peut que les éloigner, et l'on
y réuissira en rendant le pays à la
culture, et creusant des canaux
larges et profonds, et batissant des
fortins, de distance en distance.
Quant aux habitans, quelques têtes
de Cheiks les soumettront bientot.

L'Egypte ne ressemble en rien
à tout ce qu'ont dit nos écrivians.
Son sol est fécond mais point
abondant—la nature ne demande
qu'à produire, mais c'est un terrein
nud et presque inculte. Ses habitans, degradés par l'esclavage, sont
retombés dans l'état des sauvages,
et n'ont gardé de la civilisation que

la

la superstition et l'intolerance re-
ligieuse. Je les ai trouvès parfaite-
ment resemblants aux nations de la
mer du sud peintes par Cook et
Forster.

Et un mot ce-pays ci n'est rien
quant au present—il n'offre que de
grands souvenirs et des vastes mais
éloignées esperances. Il ne valoit
pas la peine d'être conquis dans
l'état actuel des choses : mais si
des politiques, surtout des admini-
strateurs habiles s'en occupent dix
ans ; si dix ans nous y employons
nos soins, et nous y sacrifions ses
revenus, il devienda la plus belle
contrée de l'Europe, et produira de
grands changements dans le commerce du monde.

CHAP.

CHAP. VI.

Grand Cairo—Capitulation of Gene-
ral Belliard—Account of the Fu-
neral of General Kleber—Return
of the Army to Rosetta.

GRAND Cairo, so renowned in
history for the splendour of its pa-
laces, its magnificent buildings, and
its great extent, now presents a very
different aspect. Like the rest of
the country, it has fallen into insig-
nificance and decay, and is the
abode of ignorance and barbarism.

The Eastern people describe it as
fol-

follows: " The superb town, the holy city, the delight of the imagination, greatest among the great, whose splendour and opulence made the prophet smile."

The French army, during their stay, had very much improved it, and had placed it in a tolerable state of defence, and in a manner impregnable to the Turks, Mamelouks, or Egyptians. During our stay in the vicinity of Cairo, a caravan entered from upper Egypt.

The merchants brought with them several Circassian women, to be disposed of to the highest bidder. The grace and beauty of these Georgians has been often celebrated. The manner and costume of these to the observer, whose prejudices have been dissipated by long travel and

reflec-

reflection, are by no means singular
or unpleasing. I saw several of
these Circassians of the most elegant and animated form. They
have generally brown hair, with
black or dark blue eyes. Their features, in general, are an assemblage
of amazingly just and regular pro-
portions. The hair, which is abun-
dantly luxuriant, falls down below
the waist ; and they were constantly
using rose water, of which they are
particularly fond, and which diffuses
a delightful fragrance around them.

The capitulation of the General
Belliard, with the whole of the
enemy's force in Cairo and its vicinity, was the signal of our retrograde
march upon Rosetta. The order
of march for the three nations,
French, Turks, and English was
some-

somewhat singular. On the morning of the 29th of July the Turkish army began to move, and were immediately followed by that of the English. The march only continued a few miles on that day, when the two armies took up their position for the night. The distance between the two encampments of one mile, prevented confusion; and each army, having its left upon the Nile, fronted that of the French, now no longer hostile. Towards the close of this day, the French garrison of Cairo, preceded by their cavalry and artillery, arrived at a position marked out, being about one mile distant from the English. This order of march was punctually observed until the whole arrived at the plains, near Rosetta.

An

An immense line of boats or
germes passed, at the same time,
down the Nile, keeping itself parallel with the head of the French
columns. The leading boat, in
which was the body of General
Kleber, being distinguished by a
large black flag. It seemed as if the
French army, ever mindful of the
distinguished merit of this accomplished officer, were resolved not to
leave even his remains in this inhospitable land of barbarism.

The military honours paid at his
funeral were very splendid ; and
the account of them appear to me
worthy of insertion. After the capture of Ramaneigh, I found in one
of the officer's rooms, the printed
account here mentioned.

I will here, therefore, take an op-

L   por-

portunity of mentioning a few circumstances relative to the General
Kleber. A few days subsequent to
the capitulation of Grand Cairo, I
took the earliest opportunity of visiting the city. Its ruins are almost
without interest ; and occupied as it
is by a people, ignorant, and almost
slaves, it is in itself little worthy of
observation.

A French officer, who accompanied me, pointed out with enthu-
siasm the residence of the late Commander in Chief, Kleber—a name
held in the everlasting remembrance
of his country ; and whose military
talents, as well as unblemished
character will ever endear him to
the troops of France. It is well
known, that long previous to the
landing of the English army in
Egypt,

Egypt, General Kleber had perished by the hand of an assassin. This latter was, by birth, a Syrian; and, after the defeat of the Turkish army, by General Kleber, on the plains of Nazareth, he had pursued his way to the French head-quarters; and having arrived at Cairo, he there accomplished the fatal deed, which deprived the world of one of its greatest ornaments, and France of one of her best generals.

It has been said, that General Kleber's death had been occasioned by the enmity of Napoleon, who, envious of his high military talents, as well as of the admiration in which he was held by the French army, had instigated the Syrian to the murder.

As this accusation was never made

to us by the French in Egypt, and
never subsequently proved, it is
wrong, and certainly unjust, to ac-
cuse even our greatest enemy without cause, and thereby give him
reason of complaint against us.

At Cairo, I procured the printed
copy of the court-martial on the
Syrian, in which were minutely stat-
ed the evidences for and against
him, his condemnation, and the account of the execution which followed. It is much to be regretted
by me that this copy has been lost,
but I hope yet to recover it.

The only remnant relative to the
burial of General Kleber, and the
funeral oration, is here subjoined,
as copied from the Gazette, printed
at Cairo.

COU-

COURIER DE L'EGYPTE.

NO. 72.

Le 9 Messidor, VIIIe. Année de la République.

KAIRE.

Obsèques du Général Kleber.

" Le canon tirait de demi-heure en demi-heure, depuis l'instant où le Général en Chef Kleber avait cessé de vivre. Le 28 prairial au matin, des salves d'artillerie de la citadelle, répétées par tous les forts annoncerent que l'armée allait lui rendre les honneurs funèbres.

Le convoi partit du Quartier Général place Ezbekyeh, au bruit d'une salve du cinq pièces de canon, et d'une décharge generale de

I 3   mous-

mousqueterie, pour traverser la ville dans l'ordre suivant, et aller deposer les restes du Général dans le camp retranché, désigné sous le nom d'Ibrahym-Bey.

Un détachement de cavalerie formant l'avant garde.

Cinque pièces d'artillerie de campagne.

Le vingt-deuxieme demi-brigade d'infanterie légère.

Le premier régiment de cavalerie de l'armée.

Les guides à pied.

Les différentes musiques de la garnison, exécutant tour-à-tour des morceaux analogues à cette triste ceremonie.

Le corps du Général Kleber, renfermé dans un cercueil de plomb, était porté sur un char funéraire

d'une

d'une belle forme, recouvert d'un tapis de velours noir, parsemé de larmes d'argent, entouré de trophées d'armes surmonté du casque et de l'épée du Général, et traîné lentement par six chevaux drapés en noir et panachés en blanc.

Le Général en Chef Menou, marchait immediatement après le char qui etait environné des généraux de l'Etat-Major Général, et précédé des aid-de-camp du Général Kleber.

Venaient ensuite le Général Commandant de la place et son etat-major.

Le Corps du Génie.

Les Membres de l'Institut.

Les Commissaires des Guerres.

Les Officiers de Santé.

Les Administrations.

Le

Le Corps des Guides à Cheval.

Hassein Kachef, Commissaire, de Mourad-Bey, accompagné de ses Mamlouks.

Les Aghas, le Kady, les Cheyks et U'lemas.

Les Evêques, Prêtres et Moines grecs.

Les Coptes et Catholiques.

Les différentes Corporations de la Ville.

Le neuvième demi-brigade.

Le treizième demi-brigade.

La Marine.

Les Sapeurs.

Les Aérostiers.

Les Dromedaires.

L'Artillerie à pied.

Le Bataillon Grec.

Les Milices Coptes.

Les Corps de Cavalerie.

Les

Les Mamlouks et Syriens à Cheval.

Un détachement, de Cavalerie française fermait la marche.

Le convoi arrivait à onze heures sur l'esplanade du fort de l'Institut; les troupes s'y developèrent en executant plusieurs manœuvres qui furent suivies d'une décharge de cinq pièces de canon, et de toute la mousqueterie.

Le char, suivi, environné, et précédé, comme ci-dessus, s'avança vers le camp retranché.

On avait ouvert une brèche sur la face du bastion nord de la couronne d'Ibrahym-Bey, pour penétrér plus directement dans la gorge du bastion, au centre de laquelle on avoit éléve la terre; le fut au milieu de cette enceinte, que

l'on

l'on déposa le corps du Général, sur un socle, entouré de candélabres de forme antique.

L'Etat-Major Général mit pied a terre pour saluter les restes du Général—les militaires de toutes les armes, de tous les grades s'avancèrent spontanément en foule, et jettèrent sur le tombeau des colonnes de cypresse et de lauriers, en accompagnant ce dernier hommage des accens vrais et flatteurs de leurs regrets.

Alors le Citoyen Fourier, Commissaire Français pres du Divan, çhargè par le Général en Chef d'exprimer dans ce jour la douleur commune, alla se placer, environné par l'Etat-Major, des grand officiers, civiles et militaires du Kaire, sur un bastion qui dominait l'armée rangée

en

en bataille, et d'une voix émue, par
la sensibilité, il prononçait le dis-
cours suivant :

Français,

Au milieu de ces apprêts fune-
raires, témoignages fugitifs, mais
sinceres, de la douleur publique, je
viens rappeler un nom qui vous est
cher, et que l'histoire a deja placé
dans ses fastes. Trois jours ne se
sont point écoulés, depuis que vous
avez perdu Kleber, Général en Chef
de l'armée Française en Orient. Cet
homme que la mort à tant de fois
respecté dans les combats, dont les
faits militaires ont retenti sur les
rives du Rhin, du Jourdain, et du
Nil, vient de périr sans défense sous
les coups d'un assassin.

I 6   Lors-

Lorsque vous jetterez désormais les yeux sur cette place dont les flammes ont presque entierement dévoré l'enceinte, et qu'au milieu de ces decombres, qui attesteront long-temps les ravages d'une guerre terrible et nécessaire vous appercevrez cette maison isolée qui cent Français ont soutenu, pendant deux jours entiers, tous les efforts d'une capitale révoltée, ceux des Mamlouks et des Ottomans; vos regards s'arrêteront, malgré vous, sur le lieu fatal où le poignard a tranché les jours du vainqueur de Maestritck et d'Heliopolis.

Vous direz: c'est là qu'a succombé notre chef et notre ami. Sa voix tout-à-coup anéantie n'a pu nous appeler a son secours. Oh! combien de bras en effet se seraient levés pour

pour sa defense ; combien de vous eussent aspiré a l'honneur de se jetter entre lui et son assassin. Je vous. prends à témoin intrépide cavalerie qui accourûtes pour le sauver sur les hauteurs de Koraïm, et dissipates en un instant la multitude d'ennemis qui l'avoient enveloppé. Cette vie qu'il devait a votre courage, il vient de la perdre par une confiance excessive qui le portait à éloigner ses gardes, et à déposer ses armes.

Apres qu'il éut expulsé de l'Egypte, les troupes de Youseph Pacha, Grand Visir de la Porte, il vit fuir ou tomber à ses pieds, les séditieux, les traîtres, ou les ingrats. C'est alorsque détestant la cruautes, qui signalent les victoires de l'Orient, il jura d'honorer par la clémence

mence le nom Français, qu'il venait
d'illustrer par les armes ; il observa
religieusement cette promesse, et ne
connut point de coupables—Aucun
d'eux n'a péri, le vainqueur seul ex-
pire au milieu de ses trophées. Ni
la fidélité de ses gardes, ni cette
contenance noble et martiale, ni
le zèle sincère de tant de soldats qui
le cherissaient, n'ont pu le garantér
de cette mort deplorable.

Voila donc le terme d'une si belle,
et si honorable carriere ! c'est la
qu'aboutissent tant de travaux, de
dangers, et de services eclatans.

Un homme agit par la sombre
fureur de fanatisme, et désigné dans
la Syrie par les chefs de l'armée
vaincue, pour commettre l'assasinat
du General Français ; il traverse ra-
pide-

pidement le désert, il suit pendant
un mois sa victime, pendant un
mois, l'occasion fatale se presente.

Negociateurs sans foi, generaux
sans courage, ce crime vous appar-
tient ; il sera aussi connu que votre
defaite. Les Français vous ont livré
leurs places sur la foi des traites.
Vous touchiez aux portes de la
capitale, lorsque les Anglois ont re-
fusé d'ouvrir la mer : alors vous
avez exigé des Français qu'ils exé-
cutassent un traité que vos alliés
avoient rompu, vous leur avez
offert le desert pour asyle. L'honneur, le peril, l'indignation ont en-
flammé tous les courages ; en trois
jours, vos armées ont eté dissipées
et détruites : vous avez perdu trois
camps et plus de soixante pièces de
canon ; vous avez été forcés d'aban-
donner

donner toutes les villes et les forts,
depuis Damiette jusqu'au Saïd. La
seule modération du Général Français a prolongé le siege de Kaire,
ville malheureuse, où vous avez
laissé repandre le sang des hommes desarmés.

Vous avez vu se disperser ou ex-
pirer dans les déserts cette multitude de soldats rassemblés du fond
de l'Asie; alors vous avez confié
votre vengeance à un assassin.

Mais quel secours, citoyens, nos
ennemis attendent-ils de ce forfait?
En frappant ce Général victorieux,
ont ils cru dissiper les soldats qui
lui obeissaient? et si une main
abjecte suffit pour faire verser tant
de pleurs, pourrat-elle émpecher
que l'armée Français ne soit com-
mandée par une chef digne d'elle:
non.

non, sans doute ; et s'il faut dans ces circonstances plus que des vertus ordinaires, si pour recevoir le fardeau de cette mémorable entreprise, il faut un esprit élevé qu'aucun préjugé ne peut atteindre, un dévouement sans réserve à la gloire de sa nation, soldats, vous trouverez ces qualités réunies dans son successeur.

Il possédait l'estime de Napoléon et de Kleber ; il leur succède aujourd'hui : ainsi, il n'y aura aucune interruption, ni dans les honorables espérances des Français, ni dans le désespoir de leurs ennemis.

— — — Le tems viendra Guerriers, estimables, quand vous vous entretiendrez, de cette contrée l'ointaine que vous avez deux fois conquise, et des armées inombrables

brables que vous avez détruites, soit
que la prévoyante audace de Napoléon aille les chercer jusques dans
la Syrie, soit que l'invincible courage de Kleber les dissipe dans la
cœur même de l'Egypte.

Que de glorieux et de touchans
souvenirs vous aurez à reporter dans
le sein de vos familles. Puissent-
elles jouir d'un bonheur, qui
adoucisse l'amertume de vos regrets !
Vous mêlerez souvent à vos récits le
nom chéri de Kleber : vous ne le pro-
noncerez jamais sans être attendrit,
et vous direz : il était l'ami et le
compagnon des soldats, il ménageait
leur sang, il diminuait leurs souf-
frances.

Vous tous Français, qu'un sort
commun rassemble sur cette terre
étrangere, vos hommages s'addres-
sent aussi, dans cette journée, aux
braves

braves, qui dans les champs de la Syrie, d'Aboukir, et d'Héliopolis, ont tourné vers la France, leurs derniers regards et leurs dernières pensées.

Soyez honoré dans ces obsèques, vous qu'une amitié particulière unissait à Kleber, ô Caffarelli, modèle de désinteréssement et de vertus, si compatissant pour les autres, si stoïque pour vous-même.

Et vous, Kleber, objet illustre, et dirai-je infortuné de cette cérémonie, qui n'est suivie d'aucune autre, reposez en paix, ombre magnanime et chérie, au milieu des monumens de la gloire et des arts !

Habitez une terre depuis si long-temps celebré que votre nom s'unisse a ceux de Germanicus, de Titus, de

Pompée,

Pompée, et de tant des grands Capitaines et de Sages qui ont laissé, ainsi que vous dans cette contrée la gloire de leurs noms.

CHAP. VII.

Conduct of a French Officer—Surren-
der of Alexandria—Pompey's Pil-
lar—Tower of Pharos—Ruins of
Alexandria.

DURING the stay of the French
army at Rosetta, the officers of the
two nations frequently visited each
other. On one of these occasions,
having dined with the Chef de Brigade, whose name, I believe, was
De Vincent, I expressed a wish to
purchase in the camp a Turkish
tent. The French officer, with much
urbanity and good humour, immediately

diately offered his services to make
inquiries for me. These inquiries
were indeed of sincere import. A
very few days subsequent, I was
awakened, at day-break, by the arrival of a French dragoon, having
under his escort, a camel, with a
large Turkish tent, together with an
Arabian horse.

The dragoon told me he had received orders from the Chef de Brigade to leave the whole in my
possession. The generosity of the
French officer did not stop here.
In a letter, he desired my accept-
ance of the horse, tent, and camel,
and gave me prescriptions against
the prevailing disorders of the country, particularly the ophthalmia,
which he said was inevitable, if the
English army continued a long time

in

in Egypt. This last prediction was indeed but too fully verified.

I am induced to mention this instance, in grateful remembrance of so distinguished an act of kindness, as from that hour I have never seen the General de Vincent.

The French army, however impetuous in the field, possesses individuals of the most honourable and disinterested character. Nor is there by any means that want of education, which is so generally believed to be the case by many persons in this country. Illiberal prejudices toward a warlike people are unjust as they are dangerous. The public papers teem with scurrility and abusive language; and, by such means, many think perhaps to evince a greater love of their own coun-

country. It is, however, doubtless,
that much mischief is done by such
reports, and enmity and rancour
are stirred up in the breasts of foreigners against England, powerful
and splendid as her character is in
the political scale of Europe. In
fact, foreigners are now apt to look
upon English travellers with suspi-
cion, and to observe towards them a
certain reserve ; the reason is obvious.

Publications almost daily present
themselves describing with ridicule,
and sometimes in very opprobrious
terms the manners and customs of
foreigners, because they do not ex-
actly correspond with our own country. Some of these publications
speak of the manners and vices of
the French nation and of Paris, with

an unbounded confidence, although
many of the writers had not passed
more than a few weeks in that
country.

It cannot, however, I should think,
be possible that travellers who make
what is called a tour, and a tour
of only a few weeks, who during
that time pass rapidly from one town
to another, who live merely in coffee
houses and hotels, can form a just
and exact estimate of the manners,
good or bad, of so great a nation as
France.

To know a country, and to judge
of it with impartiality, we must re-
side in it not only weeks and months,
but years; we should see it in
every shape, gain admittance into
the best circles, and witness also in
a military country, the manners,

K   mode

mode of life, and discipline of their armies in the field, and in their campaigns; a hasty and uncharitable judgment of our neighbour, whether friend or enemy under any circumstances, must be unjust.

Although little has been remarked in this journal by me of the Turkish army, yet I will not altogether pass them over in silence. In Egypt, it was not the custom to admire either the discipline, the manners, or the military customs of the Turks. I will not, however, presume to find fault, certain as it is that the presence of the Turkish army had great weight and influence in dispossessing the French of Egypt.

As men, they are perhaps the finest in the world in form and regularity

gularity of beauty. This, perhaps, has in great measure resulted from the climate which they inhabit, the food on which they subsist, and the nature of their occupations.

The Turk is seldom troubled either by avarice or ambition ; his mind is seldom governed by phantoms of intrigue, and he is a stranger to envy, which withers and torments the mind and body ; and to the sciences, the pursuit of which is almost always injurious to health. The Turks live on plain and healthy food ; this, together with the purity of the air which he breathes, invigorates his muscular powers. The Turkish janissary walks with a firm and manly step, and looks around him with the dignity of a Colossus.

It is extremely probable, that

Turks also possess usually that noble
form from another cause; namely,
the mode of their dress. They walk
with bare legs; and when their
cloaks are held up, their muscles
appear to swell with boldness. Their
arms are robust like those of wrest-
lers. Their necks being never con-
strained with bandages, assume the
fine proportion which nature has
designed for them. The Turkish
soldier wears no girt or bandage,
except a sash round the waist, a practice invariable in all hot countries.
In a word, all their limbs being un-
embarrassed by those bands which
impede our motions, and which nothing but habit could make us endure, preserve each its natural form,
and display those admirable pro-
portions, the perfection of which,

constitutes

constitutes the summit of human beauty. The general deportment of the Turk surpasses all other men ; a certain dignity animates, and at the same time composes their motions. Strength and gravity are displayed in their gestures ; an air of majesty which glows on their forehead, shews that they are accustomed to command.

I have never observed meanness in the look of a Turkish soldier ; pride and severity more frequently predominate, and more particularly when in the presence of Christians.

I have seen Turks, and sometimes Arabs, above sixty years of age, with the most beautiful and regular teeth. Although age has pursued

K 3   and

and overtaken them, yet their health has continued firm and vigorous.

All these advantages, however, do not intirely result from the habits of the individual.

He owes no hereditary disease to the intemperance, gluttony, or irregularity of his progenitors ; no pernicious habits, the offspring of indolence and luxury, to which the more refined Christian is subject.

The division of the army from Cairo, joined the lines before Alexandria, immediately after the embarkation of the French army.

In these lines were the regiments of guards, and a brigade of the line, all of which had continued there since the first landing, together with a considerable reinforcement which had arrived from England.

In

In the course of a few weeks after this period, General Menou finding himself closely pressed, capitulated in Alexandria, and left Egypt in possession of the English and Turkish armies.

To the westward of Alexandria, situated on an elevated ground, and distant about four furlongs, is the pillar raised to the memory of the Roman General, called the pillar of Pompey; according to some, the original pillar of that name has been destroyed, and that which now exists, is of Septimius Severus. It is still uninjured and beautiful.

Time which has here with iron despotism, destroyed so many monuments of antiquity, seems unwilling to overthrow this memorial of the great and unfortunate.

We

We could not behold this extraordinary pillar, but with respect and
satisfaction.

Even Cæsar, his powerful and
victorious enemy, wept, on beholding the murdered body of Pompey ;
how much more then had they
cause for remorse, in basely insti-
gating an assassin to destroy a man
who had so often led the Roman
armies to conquest, and added so
many wreaths of glory to imperial
Rome.

Hic linis, nomen ubique.

Beyond our encampment at the
pillar of Pompey, is the fort of
Marabou, celebrated as the spot,
where the troops of the army of
Napoleon

Napoleon effected their first debarkation.

About six leagues from Alexandria is an Arabian tower, which might be made a place of some strength; it is of very ancient construction, and appeared before we reached it, to resemble a bastion. In this vicinity, history places the ancient Taposiris, and the tomb of Osiris. All this coast, was in ages back, well inhabited, containing cities, towns, and well inhabited countries. From this tower, at the present day, the eye discovers to the north, the inconstant element the sea; and to the south and west, nothing but a void still more discouraging, of sterile sands, without even a solitary house or tree, a boundless horizon of barrenness.

Returning

Returning from hence to the city of Alexandria, we pass through the ruins of the former city of the Arabs. The circumvallation is still remarkable; but where the houses formerly stood, are now gardens, containing only a few vegetables and date trees, which collectively make but a sorry appearance: under the ruins, several individuals found various descriptions of medals, two of which are now in my possession, one of the Emperor Aurelian, and another which cannot be decyphered.

Every garden has a small cistern or reservoir of water at its gate, for the accommodation of the wearied traveller, who when arriving from the desert after a toilsome march, is here permitted to allay his thirst. They alone who have experienced the

the sensation of extreme thirst in the land of Egypt, can form a just estimate of the value of so benevolent a custom.

The whole of this part of Alexandria, is more particularly commanded by the strong and almost impregnable forts Caffarelli and Cretin, which are situated on hills, and fortified by the French engineers whose names they bear.

The obelisk called Cleopatra's needle is still beautiful and remarkable, and would have afforded an ornament of no inconsiderable import in England, had circumstances permitted its removal to that country.

This, however, was by some means or other prevented, as I know it was at one time intended by the

general

general commanding, to cause it to
be embarked for that purpose.

A second obelisk is thrown down
by its side, which in all probability
decorated one of the sumptuous
buildings in the days of the royal
founder.

On every side are discovered the
ruins of various edifices, either
Arabian or Roman, particularly a
mosque, formerly a church, dedi-
cated to St. Athanasius ; in this
mosque are innumerable hieroglyphi-
cal figures ; a very large Sarcopha-
gus was discovered by an English
officer, and near it three upright
columns partly sunk in the ground,
of very curious workmanship : passing through the extensive burial
ground, which is situated beyond
the present city, we are surprised at
its

its extraordinary appearance; innumerable marble tombs, some of them very curiously decorated, are seen on all sides; amongst these monuments of the dead, at whatever time of the day you may pass that way, many poor and meagre women are seen to wander in a singular manner.

Clad in their long garments, they resemble so many spectres, and their silence is scarcely ever interrupted. The appearance of these women lamenting over the graves of the departed, conveys a melancholy gloom to the whole scene. On quitting the burial ground, we pass near a range of Arab houses, and arrive at the Chauseè leading to the Tower of Pharos.

This Chauseè is narrow, and supported

ported by a high wall on each side; it continues for near half a mile into the sea, at the extremity of which is the celebrated Pharos, well known as the point at which Julius Cæsar nearly lost his life. The Pharos fortified by the French, is flanked with four bastions, on which some heavy guns are mounted. My regiment in consequence of the plague being apprehended in the town, remained in quarters here six weeks, and found themselves well situated.

I had before neglected to mention, that the Commander in Chief of the expedition, Lieut. General Sir Ralph Abercrombie, who was mortally wounded at the battle of Alexandria, died on the following day.

It

It must clearly appear to every
one that his loss, at such a period,
was seriously to be deplored, as his
fate was universally regretted by
every individual under his command. His death withered the lau-
rels of victory. He was a man of
mild and virtuous manners, an able
officer, possessed of the greatest
experience, and of heroic valour in
the day of battle.

The French General of Cavalry
Roize, was killed about the same
time with the English Commander,
whilst leading a charge of cavalry.
He was said to be an officer of estimation in the French army. In
his pocket were found the orders
for attack given by the General
Menou.

COPY

COPY OF THE ORDER OF BATTLE,
ISSUED BY THE FRENCH COM-
MANDER IN CHIEF THE GE-
NERAL MENOU.

General Orders.

Head-Quarters, Alexandria,
20 March, 1801.

The army will attack the English
to-morrow.

The whole of the troops will, in
consequence, be under arms at
three o'clock precisely, without
beat of drum, or any kind of noise
whatever, at two hundred paces,
in front of the present camp, beyond
the gate of Rosetta.

The general attack will commence an hour and a half before
day-break, that is to say, at half
past four o'clock.

The

The French army will be formed as follows:

The division Regnier, composed of the 15th and 85th demi-brigades, will incline its right towards the bridge upon the canal of Alexandria, in front of the camp.

The division Friant, composed of the 25th, 61st, and 75th demi-brigades, will be on the left of the division Regnier.

To the left of the division Friant, and consequently to the center, will be the column under the command of General D'Estaign, composed of the 21st demi-brigade, two companies of the 25th and the Greek grenadiers. This column is intended for the advanced guard.

To the left of the column D'Estaign, will be the division Rampon, composed of the 32d demi-

demi-brigade, and of three companies of carabiniers, belonging to
the second light battalion. This,
conjointly, with the column of
D'Estaign, will form the center of
the army.

The division of Lanusse, composed of the 4th, 18th, 69th, and
88th demi-brigades, will be to the
left of the division Rampon, and
will extend its left to the sea.

It results from this order, that
the divisions of Generals Regnier
and Friant, will form the right wing,
the divisions of D'Estaign and Rampon the center, and the divisions
of Lanusse the left wing of the
army.

A light corps will commence a
false attack upon the left of the
enemy, at the same time that the
real attack begins. This corps will
be

be composed of the corps of dromedaries and thirty dragoons.

Three hundred cavalry will be on the right of the army, beyond the canal, to annoy the enemy by continually throwing sharp shooters in front. This manœuvre will commence with the false attack made by the dromedary corps, and they will be under the orders of General Regnier.

The remainder of the cavalry of the army will be in rear of the center.

The artillery of reserve will be in the rear of the cavalry, and in their rear will be the heavy ordnance.

The grand attack will be made by the right wing of the army, under the command of the General Lanusse, and by the centre, commanded

manded by Generals Rampon and D'Estaign; they will advance to the English redoubt in front of their position, and carry it by the bayonet. At the same time the right wing of the army, commanded by General Regnier, will refuse itself at first, until the left of the army be warmly engaged. The center will support the left. The right will then advance rapidly, attacking and overthrowing every thing that it finds opposed to it.

When the position on the right and center of the enemy are carried, and all the first line broken, it will perhaps be necessary, that the French army should form again for the attack of their second line, the riflemen alone excepted.

This

This movement upon the second line of the enemy will be commenced by the left wing, which will keep back a little its right, endeavouring to turn the flank of the enemy. The center will follow this movement, and the right wing will keep in check the whole of the enemy's left.

The design of this movement is to drive the English into Lake Maadie.

General Roize, commanding the cavalry, will watch every movement of the enemy, and take advantage of every favorable circumstance, as well as the nature of the ground, to advance and destroy all that have been thrown into confusion by the infantry.

General

General Jongie will be attentive to employ the artillery usefully. It will be necessary to keep an eye on the gun-boats on the flanks of the enemy, and perhaps even that he should disperse them with some twelve-pounders.

The Generals of division will form the heads of their columns, as well as their second line, in the manner which they shall judge most to advantage.

The General in Chief will be at every point to give the necessary orders as new circumstances may arise.

MENOU—General in Chief.
LA GRANGE—Chief of the Staff.

CHAP

CHAP. VIII.

Departure from Egypt—Syracuse—
Monastery — Description of the
Country.

HAVING witnessed the embarkation of nearly the whole of the
army for England, my regiment received the unwelcome intelligence
of its destination to remain in garrison in Alexandria.

The prospect was indeed discouraging—to bear up another year
against the maladies with which
this climate is pregnant; to live
amongst Mahometans, who detested
the

the very sight of Christians, and who had already began to shew symptoms of hostile conduct towards us, will sufficiently explain the cause of our chagrin.

It was in vain to cherish useless regrets. Fortunately our bondage was of short duration. An order at length arrived for our return to Europe, and with a favourable breeze we left the shores of Africa. We sometimes derive greater advantages from the severities than from the favours of fortune. After again beholding the beautiful and stupendous buildings of Malta; after viewing with an eye of desire its amusements, I murmured against the favourable winds which forced us from them; but since I have visited the smiling shores, and become

ac-

acquainted with the inhabitants of
Syracuse, I have no cause to regret
the violence of the winds and waves,
which obliged us to delay our destined voyage to Gibraltar.

The fatigues, the cares, and the
recollections of Egypt were quickly
dissipated. At such periods of our
existence unpleasing objects and
events seldom make a lasting or
deep impression. We forget the
past, enjoy the present, and anti-
cipate the future.

On the 30th of December we
entered through stress of weather
the harbour of Syracuse.

The antient city of Syracuse was
of very considerable extent, and according to tradition equalled eighteen miles in circumference. It
was fortified according to the mode

L   and

and usages of those days, and being
contiguous to the sea, was the more
easily rendered strong and almost
impregnable.

The wars which it sustained are
well known by every reader of history, and the valour of its defenders,
has in several instances, been almost
unparalleled, and unequalled by
any other city.

At some distance from the present city are the ruins of the antient
Neapolis. Many vestiges of large
pillars of marble attest its former
magnificence. One spot, an exca-
vation of singular appearance, in-
titled the Cave or Ear of Dionysius,
is shewn to you; and, as a monument of history, as well as from its
peculiarity, is well worth the observation of travellers.

This

This cave is twenty feet in breadth, and sixty-five in heighth. It penetrates deep into the rock, and has been rendered smooth by workmanship, resembling in some measure a Gothic arch.

In the middle of the cave is a recess, the formation of which causes that extraordinary vibration, by which the smallest noise or whisper can be distinctly heard from one end to the other of the cave. The antients attribute the construction of this singular cave to the tyranny and oppression of Dionysius, who conveyed here his criminals and state prisoners. The conversation of these unhappy men could here be overheard by his guards, and immediate vengeance taken upon those who might complain

plain

plain of the severity of their lot, or divulge secrets hostile to the ty-. rant.

The country in the environs is truly delightful. Although we had quitted so lately on the plains of Gizah the reputed scite of the Elysian Fields, they by no means bear analogy to that imaginary paradise; rather, in these regions, it may be permitted to call to recollection the words of the poet:

Devênere locos lætos, et amena fricta
Fortunatorum nemorum, sedesque beatas;
Largior hic campus Æther, et lumine vestit,
Purpureo, solemque suum sua sidera norint.

In the delightful and instructive occupation of researches in such scenes, days, weeks, and months glide away imperceptibly.

The

The monuments of classical antiquity awaken the most pleasing recollections. The fatigue sometimes unavoidably experienced under the influence of a sultry climate, is nevertheless amply remunerated in the delightful environs of Syracuse, and the serene and gentle breezes from the West refresh and support him. At every step the traveller here wanders over classic ground. I was delighted to avail myself of an early occasion to visit the abode of Archimedes, the country rendered celebrated by the acts of Dionysius, and a city which had withstood so nobly the assaults of her numerous enemies.

On a small island immediately opposite to Syracuse, are the remains of an antient temple, dedi-

cated

cated to Jupiter. Two columns of granite, of considerable bulk and height, are the chief relics. From this spot Syracuse appears to advantage, and even remarkable ; beyond it, in a North West direction, is a range of hills, or rather mountains, covered by large woods, which at this distance seem to overshadow the town. A small narrow isthmus, almost connecting the island to Syracuse, is embellished with an avenue of very lofty trees, and produces a very pleasing appearance.

The temple was formerly decorated with the spoils of the Carthaginians, who in vain attempted the conquest of Syracuse, and nearly all perished by a pestilential fever. Farther to the southward is an antient monument, called l'Aquila. When

When Marcellus conquered Syracuse, the Roman soldiers are supposed to have erected it in comme-
moration of the victory.

It is situated very near the beach,
and its construction is of large massy
stones heaped, without much attention
to architecture, one upon another.

From that epoch may be dated
the bondage of the Syracusans.
A long and inglorious peace un-
nerved the discipline of their regular troops, accelerated their downfall, and was afterwards followed by
the tyranny of Verres, and other
Roman Governors.

Not far distant from the city is
the celebrated fountain of Arethusa. It now possesses only a name,
whatever may have been its former
claims to beauty and splendour.

Cicero,

Cicero, who has written so largely relative to Syracuse, uses the following words on the subject of this fountain :

" In hac insulâ extrema est fons aquæ dulcis, cui nomen Arethusa est, incredibili magnitudine plenissimus piscium, qui fluctu totus operiretùr nisi munitione, ac mole lapidum a mari disjunctus esset."

If, however, the fountain of Arethusa is no more, the enchanting scenery of its environs still exists. The climate of these happy regions still possesses its benign influence, and affords to its inhabitants abundant health, together with a flow of spirits, next in value to that first of blessings. To the charms of the climate, other advantages are joined, which augment their value, there are

are scarce any morasses in this part of the world. The waters never stand stagnate. They flow in numberless streams from the tops of the mountain, which surround the fountain of Arethusa, and form here and there small rivers, which empty themselves into the sea.

Sicily is not infested like Egypt with those clouds of insects, which swarm in the houses, and whose sting is insufferably painful and troublesome; nor is the atmosphere here loaded with those noxious vapours which arise from marshy ground. The mountains and hills are overspread with various kinds of thyme, and with a multitude of odoriferous and balsamic plants; some of the finest honey in the world is produced here.

In

In the early part of the morning there arises from the hills and vales clouds of exquisite perfumes, which embalm the air, and diffuse a fragrance around. In the month of December, I experienced here no cold, although a long continuance in the burning sands of Egypt might well render us susceptible of every blast. Neither cold, frost, or clouds ; neither snow or cold rains here afflict the human frame. When such prevail in other countries, they tend to veil the face of nature, present to the eye a train of dreary images, and swell the heart with emotions of sorrow.

In Sicily, the constant appearance of a radiant sun cheers and animates the mind. His benign influence inspires gladness and sprightly

sprightly gaiety—add to this, under
such a climate, man is liable to
fewer diseases, enjoys more plea-
sures, and has many more means of
happiness in his power, than in
countries where cold preserves his
gloomy empire. A general urbanity
and complaisance pervades all ranks.
From the families of the Baron di
Bosche and di Nava I received the
greatest politeness and hospitality.
Indeed, almost daily, these houses
were open at that period to the
English officers who visited Syracuse.

On the hill immediately above
the town is a convent of Capuchin
Friars. Its outward appearance is
desolate.

Having arrived at the extremity
of a long cloyster, we are conducted
L 6   through

through the cemetery to an iron gate. Here we descend by a numerous flight of steps into a spacious garden, situated intirely between the rocks. These subterranean retreats are supposed to have been the excavations formed by cutting stone for the antient city. These bowers, filled with odoriferous plants and shrubs, are confined by walls or rather rocks of immense height, but which are almost intirely hid from the sight by an umbrageous foliage.

In the whole island of Sicily there is perhaps no place more beautiful, where abundant nature has more profusely diffused her various bounties. This garden, or rather gardens, are laid out with simple but exquisite taste. Flowers adorned it in in the height of luxuriance, and, though artfully arranged by the un-remitting care of its possessors, seemed planted only by the hand of nature. Fountains springing from the lofty rocks cooled the air with perpetual showers, and the summit of these walls were covered with vines and jasmins.

The fragrance of the orange blos-soms breathes along the alleys, and trees of every description afford a delightful shelter from the powerful rays of a continued and ardent sun.

In one of the niches of the wall, near the entrance of the garden, is a small marble tablet, half con-cealed, on which are inscribed the following words:

Cesi

Cosi trapassa, al trapassar d'un Giorde
Della vita mortel il fiore e il verde,
Ne perche faccia, indictro Apiil iitoino,
Si rinfiora Mai, ne se rinverde.

So fades from day to day the flower of mortal life.
It is in vain the season of spiing returns;
Life never resumes its verdure or its flowers.

If I am not mistaken, these lines
are from Tasso, but they are not
unaptly placed in this retired situation.

The hill, which towers above this
singular spot, commands a noble
prospect. We beheld a series of
rich smiling vales, villages situated
on the banks of rivulets, and in-
circled with orchards of lemon,
orange, and almond trees, together
with tufts of myrtle, which crowned
the rising hills.

The traveller finds himself agreeably

ably sheltered from the heat of
noon by the frequent woods in this
part of the country, and these extending their shade to the sides of
the road, invite to repose and conversation.

The present Syracuse, or rather
the only part of the town now existing, formerly Ortygia, is at this
moment respectable in its fortifications raised by the late King of
Spain.

The town possesses four large
gates, and is surrounded by four
wet ditches, with an equal number
of glacis, scarp and counter-scarp,
and covert way. The batteries and
an extensive line of embrasures,
correspond in every respect with
the most regular fortification. In
point, however, of artillery it is
ex-

extremely deficient, having very few guns mounted, and still fewer men to work them.

The distance from Syracuse to Messina is little more than thirty miles. The road, chiefly along the sea shore, is generally pleasing and much varied. In some places there is waste land, but other parts are highly cultivated; and we frequently find several sorts of beautiful flowers growing in the fields. The traveller very often passes through agreeable walks, regularly laid out, supported by avenues of trees, which are rendered more agreeable by the cooling breezes from the Straits of Scylla and Charybdis.

The climate at Messina is reckoned to be very salubrious, and the most

most appropriate for valetudinarians
of any part of Sicily, or even Italy.
Rain is very unfrequent—a beautiful sky, scarcely ever obscured by
a single cloud, and where fogs are
totally unknown, together with the
proximity of the sea, renders the
temperature of the air delightful.
The sirocco is also less felt here than
at any other point of the island.

The harbour of Messina is beautiful, and its situation picturesque
and interesting. A narrow ridge of
land, which forms the bason, is well
fortified; four small forts command
the entrance, and a citadel, still
more elevated, is strongly built and
constructed according to the rules
of regular fortification. Resembling in some measure the works at
Syracuse, the construction is more
for-

formidable, and presents a stronger aspect than it really possesses, from the small quantity of guns and ammunition contained within its walls.

The celebrated passage of Scylla and Charybdis, at present denominated the Faro of Messina, is seen to most advantage from the citadel.

The company at the house of the Baron di Bosco was in general brilliant, and the entertainment noble. There was usually a Faro-table and other games at cards. Not above one half of the company play at these games.

From this room you pass into a larger saloon for music, which was at all times excellent. Many of the visitants, but more frequently the

the gentlemen, played and sung in a superior manner.

The third room is for conversation. Here they generally assemble towards the latter part of the evening, or walk upon the terraces. The utmost urbanity and courtesy prevailed throughout, while the temperature and moderation of the climate, and that of the demeanour of the company seemed emblematical of each other.

CHAP.

CHAPTER IX.

Minorca—Mahon—Citadella— Arrival at Gibraltar.

AT length the day of our departure came when, with regret, we
were destined to leave the hospit-
able shores of Syracuse. Although
in the midst of January, a mild and
balmy climate rendered every thing
pleasing; and, together with the
friendly and polite manners of its
inhabitants, made our abode here
truly enviable. On the eleventh
day after our departure from Sicily,

cily, we arrived at the island of
Minorca. Here, in consequence of
an accident to the ship, we were
detained some days. The island of
Minorca, a name long known to
England, is situated in the Mediterranean Sea, about sixty leagues to
the southward of the coast of Cata-
lonia, in Spain. In its neighbourhood are the islands of Majorca and
Ivica. It possesses several good
towns, and in many parts of the island are seen woods of vines and
olive trees. The greatest number
are in the vicinity of Citadella,
where they are least subject to the
violent north winds, which withers
and sensibly affects them.

The principal town, Mahon, is
situated near the harbour, and is
protected by St. Philip's castle, the
only

only fortress of note or consideration in the country. Numerous
bulwarks stretch themselves to the
shore on either side. The body of
the place consists of four bastions,
and as many curtains, surrounded
with a deep ditch, hewn out of the
solid rock. Over the roofs of the
arched buildings is a spacious and
well built rampart. The bastions
have guns mounted upon them.

The whole body of the place is
undermined, and very serviceable
subterranean works are contrived in
the rock. Before the entrance of
the Castle is a horn-work, with other
out-works to this and the remainder
of the fronts. The guns mounted towards the harbour are numerous,
and in a good state. Indeed such
is the strength of the castle of St.
Philip,

Philip, that a very considerable garrison would be required to serve it against a regular attack. Here also are capacious galleries, which are hewn out of the rock, resembling in some measure those at Gibraltar.

The troops, during a siege, however violent, are secure in those recesses from shot and shell. They may work the guns, and repose themselves in these excellent casements, without apprehension or danger.

On the point of land to the eastward is Fort Charles. It is only remarkable for the grand battery, which lies down at the water's edge. The gunners are protected by a high rampart of stone, and fire through a long range of embrasures.

The road, leading from Mahon to Cita-

Citadella or Ciudadella, is much varied. At the distance of two miles from the former it becomes very pleasant. Myrtles grow here with peculiar luxuriance. The blossoms of these afford the richest food to the bees, and produce the excellent honey, for which Minorca is celebrated. Citadella is but moderately fortified, and is not considered as a rallying point in case of a general attack upon the island. It is however surrounded by a ditch, and cut to a very considerable depth in the solid rock in some places, with the parapet of a covered way before it.

In Citadella is a large cathedral, the only one in the island. It is a noble gothic pile ; and is supposed

to

to have been built by Alphonso,
king of Arragon. A. D. 1227.

The heat in the island of Minorca
during the summer is very great. It
is then that every one gladly runs
to the sequestered cloysters of the
monasteries. The monks, in consequence of their supine and inert
life, to which destiny has made them
subject, are seen now and then to
issue from their cells in listless indolence. Their wan, and pallid looks,
proclaim their want of health, which
their poorer neighbour, the hardy
Muleteer, exposed as he is to daily
toil, under a burning sun, enjoys
with mirth and gladness.

In Mahon are several convents
and nunneries, the most considerable of which is the Franciscan.

M   Through-

Throughout the island of Minorca, we do not find traces of Roman ruins, or even the Roman road.

History nevertheless informs us, that it continued in subjection to that people from the conquest of Quintus Cecilius Metellus, one hundred and twenty-one years before the birth of Christ, to the year four hundred and twenty-one of the Christian era, when it was subdued by the Vandals, under their King Gonderia.

We left Minorca, and passed near the islands of Majorca and Ivica. I would gladly have visited them had circumstances and occasion permitted me.

On the 20th of February, we arrived in sight of Gibraltar, when, at a considerable distance, the wind being

being strong against us, the report of minute guns announced to us the death of some man of rank. These continued for some considerable time; and we were soon afterwards acquainted, by the master of a vessel, that the funeral of the Governor General O'Hara had taken place that morning.

It may be superfluous here to speak much of the rock of Gibraltar, a place so well known by various narratives, and of which so many singular accounts have been written. It is in every respect remarkable, whether as a fortress of extraordinary natural strength, and rendered still more impregnable by care and art, as from its importance in a political point of view. I was resolved to make the most of my time here;

and

and, as the peace afforded a favourable occasion to travel into Spain,
no time was to be lost in pursuing
this desirable object.

For this purpose, the most necessary preparatory step is a knowledge
of the Spanish language. The desire of seeing foreign countries is
almost universal, but the necessity
of knowing the language of the
country which travellers propose to
see, is often but too little considered by them. According to Lord
Bacon, " he that proceeds to a foreign country, without first having
an entrance into the language, goeth
to school and not to travel."

In obedience to this precept, it
was necessary to pursue with assiduity the Spanish ; and, on many
subsequent occasions, both in Spain
and

and Gibraltar, have I every reason to be pleased with that circumstance.

During the stay of the regiment at Gibraltar, I made many excursions into Spain; in one of which, in Andalusia, I had an opportunity to make some few observations on the country, manners, and customs of this particular province.

The road from Gibraltar to the Spanish lines, and from thence to Santa Roque, is by no means interesting. Turning to the left, after quitting the Spanish lines, the road passes through the orange, groves, and continues along the coast of Algeziras. Having previously been presented to the Spanish General, Don Francisco Xavier de Castanos, I had the honour to dine with him, and afterwards received from him

M 3   the

the necessary passport to proceed
into Andalusia. The bravery and
military talents of General Castanos are well known ; and his attention on this, and every other occasion, to officers from the garrison of
Gibraltar was at all times remarkable. Having arrived at the elevated position of Santa Roque, a more
pleasing prospect opens itself to the
inquiring eye of the traveller. Immediately upon descending the hills
from that town, a wild and ro-
mantic scenery is discovered.

We proceed along a road in to-
lerably good condition, until the
entrance into an extensive wood of
cork trees. In this wood, a road
has been cut sufficiently large to
admit of a carriage of four wheels.
The trees, in general, are lofty and
um-

umbrageous, which, in the sultry
month of June, afforded us the
greatest refreshment, and we proceeded on in this agreeable shade
for several miles.

On the skirts of this wood is a
village some considerable distance
from any road. It is situated in a
valley upon the bank of a rivulet.
Orange trees surround it in vast pro-
fusion. The appearance of the
country is sweet and tranquil, and
bears analogy to the mild and re-
gulated manners of its peaceful inhabitants. Having taken the direction, or rather turned our horses'
heads towards Cadiz, for the purpose of visiting the castle of Andalusia, we at length quitted the
wood, which is several leagues in
length, and arrived at the foot of

the

the mountains on which are situated
the remains of the castle. The
ruins gradually rise before us as we
advance. They appear on the
mountains like towers one after
another, which perhaps were only
divisions of the same fortress; some
of them are completely in ruins,
while others are in a sufficient state
to afford shelter; of one of these
we gladly availed ourselves, and
with the muleteers, mules, and
horses, passed the night in profound
repose.

The Spanish muleteer is one of
the hardiest and happiest of beings;
always on foot; he kept pace with
our horses, and amusing himself continually with some national air; he
never appeared tired or exhausted
from the length of the journey, or
the

the intense heat of the sun; he accordingly at day light every morning was ever at his post, and remind-
ed us of the necessity of pursuing
our journey.

The plain into which we afterwards descend, becomes wild in
about a league. It opens circular-
ly, being bounded on all sides by
prodigiously high mountains; neither in the neighbourhood of Marmorice in Asia, nor in Sicily, with
the exception of Mount Ætna, have
I ever witnessed any country so ro-
mantic, so noble, or so stupendous
as that of Andalusia.

After traversing three leagues of
this plain, the country becomes
handsome and more diversified. It
is woody, with intervals of cultivation; we perceived numerous cottages,

M 5

tages, and the road at length turns
and discovers a superb curtain of
verdure formed by a chain of mountains, in the centre of which, the
turrets of a monastery of the Franciscan order begin to appear.

The convents and monasteries in
Spain, are almost without exception,
situated in beautiful parts of the
country, and attention has been
paid to select situations, where the
scenery is grand and magnificent.
The prospect here is admirable, dis-
playing at once noble and picturesque views; vineyards, gardens,
corn-fields, and fruit trees of all kinds,
appear in great abundance. The
villages in the immediate view are
admirable, and the monastery which
crowns the summits of the centre
mountain, serves to augment the interest of the agreeable landscape.

Having

Having passed the night at a neighbouring posada, we took the earliest opportunity of visiting the monastery.

On asking if it might be permitted to enter the gates without infringing upon the rules of the order, the monk who came to the gate informed us, that the superior was at all times willing to receive travellers; but if foreigners, he should be still more gratified in shewing them attention and respect.

Over the inner gate-way are inscribed the following remarkable words:

" Il n'y a point d'Asyle plus sur pour l'homme, que l'amour et la Crainte de Dieu." An air of serenity and happiness seemed to pervade this extraordinary mansion.

The

The cloysters are prolonged in parallel lines to a considerable extent. The windows of each cell has the prospect of the distant country and is protected at the same time by groves of myrtle and citron trees.

Aromatic plants of all kinds are carefully cultivated by these happy men, who seem to find in philosophy, in religion, and in a regular course of life the greatest consolations.

It does not appear that all the monks of this fraternity have entered it from early youth, and I have reason to think our conductor upon this occasion, had passed in the great world the far greater part of his existence. He was a man of mild and benignant aspect, possessing the Spanish cast of features,

tures, extremely handsome at his age of sixty years, although much burnt with the sun.

Monks in general from their still and indolent mode of life, have a swarthy and palid hue, and severe cast of features.

The cell of our conductor was particularly simple ; a large crucifix, with some books and writings, were all that could be discerned ; on the wall were written the lines as follows :

" L'homme croit trouver dans les honneurs, dans les plaisirs, et dans les richesses, des appuis et du repos que lui chappent.

" Partout it trouve des plaisirs in-suffisans ; des vuides rennuissans qui ne peuvent se semplir, et un bon-heur fugitif qui lui est montrè et appercû, ou il l'narrive jamais."

I cannot

I cannot confess myself a prose-
lyte of this doctrine, but I give it
as it is written.

Several other monks came to view
us with curiosity. I could discern
a satisfaction in these people, which
convinced me they were truly happy
men. Their manners were extremely courteous, and they evinced an
amiable and charitable disposition,
by treating us without regard to
either nation or religion with the
utmost benevolence.

The monk in speaking of his own
condition, said, " what can indeed
be wanting to a happy life at such
an age, when every thing is provided without care, when the day
may be gratefully passed away in
an innocent variety of diverting and
pleasing toils, where our repose is
never

never interrupted by anxiety for worldly affairs." " The world," he added, " misconceive, and do not understand the system of monasteries; the mode of life and occupation of its inmates, and the advantage which would naturally result from similar habits to the greater part of mankind, if instead of the uncertain and precarious cares they pursue, they would abandon as unprofitable and vexatious the troubles inevitable in public life, and seek refuge in retreats such as you here witness.

" Men in general are tormented more by the opinion they have of things, and not by the things themselves."

> Sapiens sibique imperiosus
> Quem neque pauperios neque mors
> Neque vincula terrent
> In quem manea suit semper fortuna.

In

He seemed particularly well informed respecting the topography
of all the nations of Europe, of
their manners, customs, and political influence.

He observed that the English
kept la Plaza, meaning Gibraltar,
in order to drive out of the Mediterranean the other powers of
Europe ; but that they shut in at
the same time the greatest robbers,
meaning the Algerines and the
other pirates of Barbary, for the
purpose of aiding their own interest.

The elevation of this convent is
about 200 fathoms above the level
of the sea ; that of Madrid, which
is perhaps the highest point of all
Spain, about 300 fathoms, which is
nearly equal to the defiles of the
Tyrol.

CHAP.

CHAP. XI.

Journey to Ronda—Town of Ronda—
Bull Feasts—Amusements—Spanish
Customs.

AT the distance of four leagues
from the Convent is the little town
of Murillo, beyond which are several forests of considerable extent.
We arrived there about eleven at
night, having left the Convent in the
evening to avoid the heat of the
weather. In passing over the mountain, which is a continued vineyard,
the lights from the town below, and
the

the sound of the guitar, which in this part of the world is to be heard in almost every cottage, afforded a pleasing variety, and dissipated the fatigues of the journey.

In Spain, after the labour of the day is passed, the song and dance, and that of no contemptible nature, are universal even in the most retired hamlets.

Dullness and stupidity seem to be forbidden. Traversing the forests above mentioned, which are sometimes difficult of passage, from the thick and luxuriant foilage, you discover several villages, surrounded with orchards and beautiful meadows. Near to this point, we took notice of a cross newly erected, and a quantity of small stones thrown around it. It was raised, I was in-

formed

formed by the muleteer, for a person there murdered, as is the custom
throughout Spain : and that every
Catholic held it his duty to cast a
stone upon the place, in abhorrence
of the fatal deed. The road from
hence is in the bed of a river, at this
time totally dried up, but which in
winter is of considerable depth.

On the banks of the river, which
passes through a deep valley for a
continuance of nearly fifteen English miles, are very large acassias,
myrtle trees of large growth, and
various species of roses.

As we wind along the bank towards the interior, we catch a
glimpse of the village of Cuenca, on
a hill, which rises in the figure of a
pyramid, and on whose summit are
the ruins of an old castle.

At

At length, from a rising ground, you descry the town of Ronda, which stands in a beautiful country, embosomed by hills. On the west and north-east, it is bounded by immense woods; and on the south, you are conducted by a good road to the gates of the town. Every thing here bespeaks a past grandeur superior to the present. Every thing announces the power of its former masters, the Moors.

The environs are very pleasant, and fertile, and abundant in trees of all species, and productions of every kind. We found at Ronda many amusements. Every evening the house of some nobleman received company, to which the English officers were invited. We found the music, particularly the band of the regi-

regiment of Tarragona, excellent.
The Spanish music, in general, is
peculiar and interesting. The dancing also of the south of Spain is of
the first description, and surpasses
most other parts of Europe.

Ronda, at this time, was crowded
with visitors, in consequence of the
toros which are held here, and are
said to be little inferior to those of
Madrid.

The toros, or bull feasts, are indeed extremely splendid at this
season at Ronda. The amphitheatre, resembling in its construction
those of Rome, contains nearly six
thousand spectators. These sit on
benches, over which is an arched
roof, the arena, the place of action,
being open to the air. About one
o'clock in the day, we perceived
large

large crowds of people entering the theatre.

Although it is an exhibition which, from its nature, is revolting to those unaccustomed to see it. As a custom of the Spaniards, I cannot, of course, presume to find fault with it; but will relate the few circumstances, attending which I this day witnessed.

It was given out that great entertainment might be expected, both from the experience and skill of the combatants, as well as from the animals, six in number, which were said to be extremely fierce and powerful, and had been driven in from the mountains on the preceding evening. These animals are by no means such as may be generally supposed, or such as we are accustomed

tomed to see in the pastures and
farm-yards of England.

Being of a very large and fierce
description, accustomed to rove in
wilds and forests, without scarcely
seeing human beings, they resemble
in ferocity beasts of prey, and excell
in strength almost all other animals.

On the evening preceding the bull
fight, I saw them pass through a
part of the town, which had been
prepared for the purpose, by placing
ropes and palings, so as to prevent
the bulls from attacking the popu-
lace, which otherwise, would have
taken place. Their approach was
announced by the sound of trumpets, which, together with the bel-
lowings of the animals, enraged at
being thus driven from their inde-
pendant domains, the plains and forests,

rests, surprised in no small degree those persons unaccustomed to such scenes.

At length they reach the Tauril, which is a dungeon or enclosure, very narrow, impervious to the light, and where they remain without food until the hour of combat.

On the upper part of the breast is fixed a riband of blue, red, or yellow colour, denoting the breed and origin of the animal, and the part of the country, from which he has been brought. Taking therefore into consideration the afore-mentioned circumstances, it will not be a matter of surprise that the Spaniards, accustomed to be fondly addicted to these diversions, should be so extremely interested in the appearance and breed of the animals,

as

as well as in the skill, courage, and activity of the men and horses employed on the occasion.

The combatants, both horse and foot, are clothed in the old costume of Spain, richly ornamented. The former wear the old Moorish saddle, and use lances of a particular fashion, and are also defended from receiving injury, by large paddings covered with leather. These surround the legs, arms, and body, and prevent the goring of the bull. The horseman is consequently seldom in danger, but from the falling of his horse, when the fracture of a limb often happens.

The piccadores, or horsemen, having taken their station on the arena, flourishes of several trumpets announce the opening of the folding

N   gates

gates of the Tauril, and the bull appears. The noble and gigantic
animal, enraged at his long and unworthy imprisonment, looks wildly
around him on the spectators, spurns
with his hoofs the ground, and sur-
veys with disdain the men and
horses, whom he has hitherto been
accustomed to despise. At this moment the attention and interest of
the spectators is wound to the highest pitch.

The piccador, on whom the bull
first rushed, held his lance in rest.
Both horse and horseman reeled
with the shock. The bull received
a wound with the spear, which is so
formed as to be prevented from pe-
netrating far into the body. He
however repeated his attack, and
was several times parried by the
skill

skill and agility of the piccador, being on every attack slightly wounded. The enraged animal now suddenly wheeling, attacked the second piccador, and dreadfully gored the flank of the horse.

The sight of this was truly horrible; the unhappy animal actually treading upon his own entrails. Still, however, he held his rider, his noble nature apparently disdaining to give way. It is also the custom that, until the horse falls, or is found to faulter from loss of blood, the piccador is not permitted to retire. The bull, now fondly exulting in seeing the distress of his enemy, whom he pressed round the arena, seemed to be impelled still further by the plaudits and loud acclamations of the spectators, vociferating

the

the words, to the charge, to the charge, which re-echoed from every part of the amphitheatre. Hundreds of handkerchiefs were seen waving in the hands of the ladies, who were equally animated with the men in urging the combat. The exertions of the second piccador, who now again attacked the bull, allowed time for the wounded horse of his companion to leave the arena.

After a very short interval, the men on foot, or banderillos, make their appearance, when the piccador resigns to them his station.

The banderillos are lightly but sumptuously dressed, in short silk cloaks of various colours. Their activity is astonishing. They pass and repass the animal, throwing small darts into his neck, and other

parts

parts of the body, which irritate and render him still more furious and indignant.

The rapidity with which he pursues is almost inconceivable; and nothing but the practice of throwing a cloak over the eyes of the animal, and springing over the outward parapet of the arena, could possibly save them. The poor animal thus cheated, vents his unavailing rage upon the cloak which remains on the arena.

The matador, who is to close the tragic scene, at length appeared, and every other combatant retired.

He held in his right hand a short stiff sword, and, in his left, a small red flag. On his skill and resolution, his activity and promptitude, depends his life. An universal si-

lence

lence succeeded to the acclamations, and the attention and hopes of the spectators redoubled. They trembled alike for the life of the man, yet seemed unwilling to resign the noble spirited animal, who deserved a better fate, yet anxious to defend his life, and still disdainful of his enemy.

The matador, having bowed to the box of the Corregidor, the governor, turned himself, reconnoitreing the movements of the bull, who now became more wily and cautious, as well as weakened by the severity of his wounds, and advanced slowly upon him, waving in his left hand the red flag. The animal, deceived by this, watched his opportunity to rush on the matador; and, in closing upon him, received the sword be-

between his shoulders, which caused immediate death.

Four mules were now brought in, richly harnessed, and whirled away with rapidity the dead body, with ropes fastened round the horns. Here the ardour, which prevailed amongst the spectators in favour of the man, suddenly changed; and, as the carcase so lately endued with vigour and courage trailed along the arena, every individual seemed to cast after it a look of pity and of admiration, and to lament a custom which deprived so noble an animal of existence.

On this occasion, six bulls were brought in successively in the same manner. Five horses were killed, and one piccador had his arm broken. The Spaniards delight in this

species

species of amusement; and, although the number of persons collected together were immense, not the least irregularity took place, nor did· I observe during my stay here, or in any other part of Spain, a single drunken man.

The abstemiousness and temperance of the Spaniards is proverbial, and is justly celebrated. The following custom may be deemed somewhat singular. If a man, upon any occasion, should be brought as an evidence against another, and it can be proved that he has ever been drunk, that circumstance will invalidate the whole evidence.

On passing from the exhibition above-mentioned, near the principal cathedral, at sun-set, the bell of the Ave Maria sounded. This sound occa-

occasioned an universal pause. The footsteps of every one were, at the same moment of time, arrested. Every being fell upon his knees, and seemed to beseech the Author of his existence. Thus, at the same point of time, every subject of the King of Spain performs an act of devotion: and finds in the Ave Maria bell, a monitor, constant and invariable.

> " Squilla di lontano
> Che paija il Giorno, pianger che si monta."

A singular practice in some parts of Spain is that of the ceremony, used at the execution of malefactors.

As they pass from the dungeon to the fatal spot, the procession invariably stops before the images of the saints, occasionally fixed at different

points

points of the streets. Here they continue some time in prayer with the Catholic clergymen, who attend them. On every occasion of this nature, it is the custom for the musicians of the city also to attend at the place of execution. On the approach of the condemned, they play the most affecting and interesting airs, adapted to the solemn occasion. This music heightens the scene of sorrow, and brings tears of compassion into the eyes of the most obdurate and unfeeling.

We attended the high mass at the Cathedral. The service was extremely interesting, and the music calculated to give the most delightful impressions to the mind. One of the attendants of the Cathedral, who had placed us in the best situation of the

the church, took his station near us,
and seemed to watch our motions
and countenances with curiosity. On
a sudden, the sound of voices, accompanied by the organ and numerous instruments, proceeded from a
distant part, and from persons who
were not seen. The effect was
equally new and gratifying. At
every instant the church became
more gloomy, by decline of day;
and the music, which was of Pa-
siello, was rendered more solemn
and interesting. It was at the period of the benediction, a few
torches only glimmered through the
long aisles and at the altar. This,
together with the pious, silent, and
respectful attitude of the people,
presented a scene equally devout
and impressive.

I have already mentioned that a

numerous

numerous assemblage of company
were then at Ronda. The Almeyda
every evening was filled with well
dressed people, and amongst them
some of the most beautiful women
in the world. The Spanish ladies,
particularly in the south of Spain,
are remarkable for their fine eyes,
noble features, a shape almost unequalled, and a graceful deportment. The dress usually worn is
black, ornamented with the richest
lace, and is highly becoming.

The town of Ronda is built upon
the declivity of a mountain or rock,
which has the appearance of having
been rent asunder, and the two divisions of the town are connected by
a bridge. The distance from this singular bridge to the abyss beneath is
astonishing. During the period that
the Moors occupied this and other
parts

parts of Spain, many monuments of architecture were constructed by them. The majestic ruins that are still scattered over many of the provinces of Spain, would be sufficient to prove that this country was once the seat of a more considerable empire, and that its government was at that time more active, more attentive to its grandeur, and more renowned for its attention to arts and arms. It is to be lamented that Spain, from the peculiarity of its local situation, is within the reach but of very few travellers, and foreigners in general are thus forbidden an intercourse with one of the most noble countries in the world.

Several of the assemblies here at the houses of the 'grandees were extremely brilliant both from the
elegance

elegance of the Spanish ladies, the superior dancing, and from the excellent music, which seems to be here almost universal.

Thus closed our very confined visit to this beautiful and fertile province of Spain. I could have wished, instead of six weeks, to have passed six months in visiting this extraordinary part of the country.

A much longer space might have agreeably been filled. On foreign ground curiosity is our business, and our pleasure; and the traveller, conscious of his ignorance, and covetous of his time, is diligent in the search and view of every object that can deserve his attention.

The character of the Spaniard is noble and disinterested, naturally brave

brave but vindictive, and sometimes arrogant and reserved. But, if his vices are considerable, they are never low and ignoble.

In the late arduous and terrible contest, the efforts made by the Spanish nation have been extraordinary, and the wonderful acts of heroism of individuals incalculable, and beyond all comparison. Very few can form an adequate idea of the sufferings and losses sustained by French armies in that country, in their desultory warfare with the Spaniards. The recent publication by a French officer of Hussars, Mons. Rocca, is the only one which describes in accurate terms the horrors of that astonishing period.

The Spanish women are more lively, animated, and interesting, both

both from the naïveté of their manners, and the charms of their beauty.
There are very few foreigners, particularly if English or French, who
do not pass the greater part of their
time with the latter, without solicit-
ing the notice or consideration of
the former.

I have been much gratified with
this short visit into Andalusia, but
have only described it with rapid
brevity. Every traveller however
who visits Spain, must be aware that
he has many obstacles to surmount,
much difficulty to overcome, and
many privations to endure. After
every tedious journey, he must not
expect to find the agreeable repose
of an inn. The word *convenience* is
utterly unknown in that country;
and, instead of meeting with the
advan-

advantages of an English or French hotel, the traveller often finds himself without the common articles of food, and obliged to sleep during the night in the same room or barn with the mules, and muleteers. Among Spaniards also, he will seek in vain for that national urbanity of France, which, from the court, has diffused its gentle influence to the camp, the cottage, and the schools.

The use of foreign travel has often been questioned and debated. The indispensable requisites of mature age and judgment, a competent knowledge of men and books, and a freedom from domestic prejudices, prevent many, who, as it is called, go abroad, but who by no means travel, from reaping any substantial advantage. Many qualifications
are

are essential to a traveller. He should be endowed with an active indefatigable vigour of mind and body, which can seize every mode of conveyance, and support, with a careless smile, every hardship of the road, the weather, or the inn. The benefits of foreign travel will correspond with the degrees of these qualifications ; and, without possessing them in an eminent degree, he will return to his native country, rather disgusted than pleased with what he has seen and experienced in others.

CHAP.

CHAP. XII.

Return to Gibraltar—Description of
the pestilential Fever in that Gar-
rison.

ON leaving Ronda, we were induced to vary our rout of return.
The valley, at the entrance of which
it is situated, is every where beautiful.   We passed through this valley, and in the evening arrived at
the village of El-Carpio. A delightful verdure covered the surrounding
hills, and abundant vineyards, cultivated even to the tops of the mountains, were scattered on all sides.
The

The road however is somewhat rugged, uneven, and steep, and the extremely narrow passes in the mountains occasion some fatigues, and would, be impassable but to mules and horses accustomed to the country. The accommodations of the Venta this evening were extremely bad.

Beyond El-Carpio, new mountains present themselves, sometimes smooth and slippery, sometimes broken and uneven, and replete with dangers to the horses and to travellers. The ascents and descents rapidly succeed each other, and the traveller is pleased to regain a more practicable route.

The journey altogether was extremely interesting; and in a few days we again reached Gibraltar.

After

After a residence of one year and a half in this garrison, in the year 1804, an order had been expected by the regiment for its return to England. This expectation, however, was never fulfilled to many, who were here doomed to finish their career, and to terminate their labours, not by the chance and fortune of warfare, but by the still more baneful and destructive enemy disease.

It will be readily imagined that I allude here to the pestilential fever, which raged amongst the ill-fated inhabitants of this place in the autumn of 1804.

Although it is nearly impossible for any one, even if possessed of the powers of an able writer, to pre-

sent

sent a faithful and adequate picture of that scene of horror and human misery; yet I will endeavour to give a brief account and some few anecdotes of several circumstances of which I was an eye-witness and near observer.

About the latter end of September, as far as my journal permits me to assert, the 24th of the month, a report reached us, that a Moorish Jew, an inhabitant of the town, had been suddenly seized with a violent fever, and had expired within forty-eight hours from his first seizure. This man had been buried in the court-yard of his house. A Roman Catholic Priest, had asserted that this man died of the pestilential disorder, similar to that of Malaga,

Malaga, which had occasioned the death of many thousands of people in the preceding year.

Unaccustomed as are the individuals of a regiment to give credit to, or to dread reports of such a nature, it was soon ascertained how much reason we had to believe the opinion of the well-informed Priest.

Every day from that unhappy period brought with it sinister accounts, and added to the list of the sick and of the dead.

At first the disorder seemed to confine chiefly its ravages to the inhabitants of the town, who died in numbers ; forty or fifty persons were seized daily. At length it extended itself to the troops, who, for the most part, were quartered in the south

south part of the rock, and partly encamped on Windmill Hill.

The 10th regiment of foot alone were encamped on the grand parade, near the town. The baneful influence of this destructive fever scarcely knew of bounds, and was repulsed by no force or skill.

It brought with it, in the first instance, excruciating pain, which was succeeded by stupor, and generally, in the rapid space of forty-eight hours, inevitable death. Let me recall a few instances, marked in my journal, within my own immediate observation:

On the 1st of October, an officer of the regiment was taken ill, and died on the third day. On the 6th of October two other officers shared the

the same fate. By the 13th of October seven officers of the regiment had died. The whole number of the officers originally present with the regiment were sixteen. Two only of those who had been seized with the fever recovered.

About this period the Governor Major General Barnard died, and a few days subsequent his Aid de Camp, Lord Pelham Clinton. The duties of the garrison now became extremely arduous and severe upon those officers, who continued in health.

During the month of October I was upon the guard or picquet every other night without exception. On one of these occasions, the subaltern officer of the Waterport guard on duty with me, reckoned ninety-eight

o   dead

dead bodies, which were carried past during the day, rolled up in blankets, and conveyed to the neutral ground, the place of interment appointed for the inhabitants.

On the following morning, when returning home with the guard, some men of the regiment were observed to be digging a grave in the officer's burial ground. These men informed us of the death of the Adjutant. In two days from this moment the officer then with me was also buried.

In respect to the town, it surpassed in horror all that can be imagined. At several points, waggons were stationed as hearses. Hither the wretched inhabitants conveyed the bodies of their relations. The unwilling burthens were

hastily

hastily thrown into these loathsome vehicles of death, which when filled, were rapidly driven away to the same neutral ground above-mentioned.

There were several instances of individuals attempting, by seclusion, to avoid the dreadful enemy, which seemed to tread upon the heels of the most wary.

One of the inhabitants in the civil employment of government, with his wife, retired to a small house on the south part of the rock. Even the servant was sent away, and a soldier carried to them daily such necessaries as were indispensable for their subsistence. Both these people died in a very short space of time, and on the same day.

o 2   In

In one house, near the main guard, in which were several Jewish families, eighteen persons died. Dead bodies were also frequently found in several houses, where they had been left shut up and unknown.

The system for the disposal of the sick was as follows :—a Lazaretto was established on the neutral ground, and an encampment formed —hither all the sick belonging to the poor families of the town, whether English, Spanish, Moors, or Jews, were conveyed.

It is impossible for any individual to form a just estimate of the numbers who died here; that they were very considerable, and even numerous, is evident from the circumstance of working parties being ordered

ordered continually from the garrison to dig a burial place. Large
pits were made of twelve feet in
depth, and proportionably broad,
into which the bodies were thrown
immediately after death. The inhabitants of the better order in
the town were permitted to remain
in it; but in case of death were conveyed, without exception, to the
same neutral ground, and buried at
the Lazaretto.

On the 15th of October, I commanded the picquet at the grand
battery. This picquet had not
been usual, but an augmentation
was deemed necessary to support
the Land-port guard in case of any
surprise. I am convinced, and do
not hesitate to say, that in the garrison at Gibraltar, at that period,

not

not more than one thousand men
of every description of troops could
be depended upon in case of emer-
gency.

Had the Spaniards at this time
been at war with England, no
doubt could be entertained of their
making an attempt against the garrison, and in which, in all probability, they would have succeeded.

In riding through the streets of the
town, and none but a few officers
ever ventured to do so, a desolation presented itself scarcely to be
imagined but by such as witnessed
its miserable effects. Dreadful
scenes, at the bare relation of which
human nature shudders, and the
sight of which impressed a melancholy horror, which can never be
effaced. Every window and door
were

were absolutely blocked up from one end of the town to the other without exception.

Occasionally from the tops of the houses, meagre and dying individuals were seen, whose faultering voices implored, generally in vain, the pity of the few passengers, who were seldom enabled to afford them relief,. even had the common danger not hardened every heart. These unhappy people often expired in their houses, and on the tops of them, where they had sought, as a last refuge, a little air; and where, after the disease had partly ceased, many were found in the most loathsome state of corruption.

The officers burial place is situated immediately beyond the town,

and

and close under the batteries of the South-port Gate.

Having one morning attended to the grave the seventh officer of the regiment, I entered South-port Gate with an intention of riding through the town. From this spot as far as the eye could penetrate to the end of the street, not a single individual could be seen. Apparently solitary, in the midst of a populous town, I saw nothing, but heard on either side a confused noise of voices, intermingled groans, and the doleful lamentations of the sick and dying. The sentinels on duty, alone seemed mindful of their usual employment, and unmindful of their danger, and of the fate which probably awaited them.

Accustomed to view perils, and
to

to undergo hardships with indiffe-
rence, they seemed cheerful amidst
the general consternation, and per-
formed every thing required of them
with alacrity.

On passing the convent, the residence of the Governor, I observed
the gates already closed. The sentinels were at their post, and after
paying the usual compliment, one
of them informed me of the death
that morning of the officer commanding the garrison, Major General Barnard. His loss at this
crisis was particularly to be lamented, and more especially so, as
his amiable character and general
demeanor had endeared him to all
under his command.

At some distance beyond the convent is the Spanish church; which
at

at the early hour I then passed, had usually been filled with people. It was in vain that upon this occasion entering it, I cast my eyes around for living objects. The feeble rays of the sacred lamp shot through the lattices and casements. An universal and melancholy stillness, emblematical of the silence of the surrounding tombs reigned throughout.

Retracing my steps, I suddenly perceived the figure of a single individual habited in a long Spanish cloak, and kneeling before a crucifix. On my near approach to him, the Spaniard raised his head, and exhibited to me a countenance, pale and emaciated from extreme want. The shades of death seemed already to have overtaken him, and
his

his eyes were absolutely sunken and
hollow.

Inquiring from him by what
means he had contrived to enter
the church, he replied in his own
language, pointing to his mouth,
that for two days he had not received food, and that for the last
three weeks he had barely sub-
sisted on the refuse found in the
streets, and by bread given him occasionally by the soldiers.

Not belonging to the town, he
had been refused admittance into
every house, and had been equally
prevented from quitting the rock.
" Every human being," he added,
" shuns me, drives me away with-
" out pity or commiseration, and
" fears that I am infected with the
" plague; it is better for me to
                " die

" die here within the holy walls
" of the church, and in the sanc-
" tuary of the Almighty." I told
him, that in an hour he should
find every thing he wanted in the
box of the sentinel contiguous to
the church door. Here he crossed
himself, continuing his devotions as
before.

This poor man, a native of Malaga, afterwards quitted Gibraltar in
good health.

Such were the horrors which
then pervaded this ill-fated place,
that the greater part of its inhabitants, timid and irresolute
through the terror of death and the
love of life, repelled from them their
nearest friends and even relations,
and refused one to another the
slightest aid or assistance.

Amongst

Amongst the soldiers a noble conduct, very dissimilar, displayed itself; and they who preserved their health, afforded the kindest offices to the unfortunate sick, regardless of every danger, and unmindful of the chances of subjecting themselves to the same unhappy disorder.

The servants of the officers in many instances, were known to lay on the ground near the bed of their masters who were ill and dying, and without quitting them during the whole process of the complaint.

In the course of fifteen days, I lost by the fever four servants successively.

A soldier, when in the capacity of a servant, and of good character, is ever attentive to the interests of his

his master. He undergoes when in the field, even hardships and privations with cheerfulness, and is unavoidably subject to more fatigues than other soldiers. After long and harassing marches, in the most inclement weather, he is obliged, instead of reposing himself, still to be employed, and he performs without a murmur and without repining, perhaps tenfold more than an ordinary servant would ever consent to do.

During the whole, or nearly the whole time of the fever at Gibraltar, its malignity was in all probability augmented, in consequence of the continued prevalence of the Levanter or easterly wind, which oppressed, and wore down without intermission, the miserable inhabitants.

The

The spring and elasticity of the atmosphere seemed to be lost, and that active principle which animates all nature, appeared to be dead.

An experiment was tried by the governor, to rouse and dissipate the incumbent air by the force and action of gunpowder, and the concussion occasioned by the firing of cannon.

For this purpose every thing having been arranged, and all the artillery-men collected, the batteries of the heaviest ordonnance were opened almost at the same period of time.

These consisted of the king's bastion, the line of guns along the line wall, the batteries which surround Waterport, the Montagu, Willis, and grand batteries, together with all the guns commanding the north front.

The

The report of three hundred pieces of cannon reverberated by the rock, and borne by the small degree of wind which blew towards the Spanish shore to Algesiras, must naturally have occasioned no little surprise to the Spaniards. They are said to have exclaimed, " Es " verdad, que todos los Ingleses, no " estan muertos."

The whole rock was thus enveloped in the smoke of gunpowder: the decomposed particles it was imagined, would have had a tendency to dissipate the putrid air. Whatsoever might have been its tendency, the influence was of short duration, and its effects transient. The disease continued to rage with unabated vigour, and every hour of the day and of the night, added to the number of the dead.

Over

Over the broad extent of the Bay, which at other times presented a lively and animated scene, and was visited daily by ships of various nations, not a vessel could be discerned, save at intervals, the small white sails of the Algerines coasting along the African shore, and who seemed to avoid us with caution and even horror.

Towards the land, and the Spanish lines, a like desert and lonely aspect presented itself; a few Spanish soldiers alone belonging to the guard room at Fort St. Philip, and occasionally a solitary sentinel above the walls were to be discovered. Over the neutral ground, now become the receptacle of the dead, we observed every morning numerous flights of birds, of vultures,

P ravens,

ravens, and sea-gulls; many of them could scarcely be driven away, and when approached very near, they frequently would fly but a few yards from the point of their first attraction.

Of all the officers at Gibraltar, and there were many who during this unhappy and dreadful period, never shrunk from the duty allotted to them, but who continually night after night were without rest, and who were the only people who occasionally assisted the miserable inhabitants, no person was more conspicuous than Captain Richard Wilson of the 2nd or Queen's Regiment.

I here deviate from my general custom in mentioning the name of this Officer. Although disease and death might be said to inhabit every

house

house and room, and to be wafted on every breeze, he was indefatigable in visiting the quarters of the officers, and the barracks of the men and hospitals. To give an idea of the numbers who died nightly in these last, I have frequently passed in the morning between twenty and thirty bodies of those who had died during the night, and were conveying to the military burial ground.

In a word, the pestilential fever at Gibraltar in the year 1804, has, I believe, equalled for the time of its continuance, the most destructive fevers experienced in the West Indies or elsewhere; and I am convinced, that a city visited by such a misfortune, presents the most frightful scene of misery known to human nature.

THE END.